# A MUSLIM'S GUIDE TO HAPPILY EVER AFTER

## A Guide For Muslims Seeking to Get Married

Foreword from Sheikh Mohammed Al-Hilli

By
Rahat Husain

**TAQWA** media™

ISBN 13: 978-1-939420-06-0 (paperback)
Library of Congress Control Number:  2014939225

Published by:
Taqwa Media LLC
Monmouth Junction, NJ
www.taqwamedia.com

Taqwa Media LLC is a print and digital publishing, marketing and distribution company. Established in September 2012, Taqwa Media's vision is to share the message of God-conciousness (taqwa) using state-of-the-art technology. Our company provides an opportunity for independent publishers and authors to disseminate their works using our global distribution network.

Printed in the United States of America

# Dedication

*In the name of God, the Beneficent, the Merciful*

*This book is created in the service of the Almighty and is dedicated to the Holy Prophet and the Lady Khadija, an example in marriage and happiness for every generation.*

*This book is also dedicated to my wonderful wife and to my amazing daughter.*

## Guiding Principle of This Book

The Holy Prophet (PBUH) says,
"No house has been built in Islam
more beloved in the sight of Allah
than through marriage."

# TABLE OF CONTENTS

# Sheikh Mohammed al-Hilli

# FOREWORD

Marriage is a subject that appeals to many people, and is arguably the most important decision any one of us makes in our lives. Given its special place in the lives of human beings, Islamic teachings have given focus on all aspects associated with this special relationship.

The focus includes pre-marital considerations, guidance on choosing the right spouse, and importantly fostering a healthy long lasting bond between the couple.

Muslim Scholars argue that this emphasis is unique within the religion of Islam, as the teachings of the Holy Prophet Mohammad (Peace Be Upon Him or 'pbuh') point to marriage being the holiest institution.

In addition to safeguarding half of one's faith, marriage is regarded as a relationship blessed by The Almighty God (swt); infused with His love and mercy.

Therefore, married couples are reminded by Islam that their sustenance will increase, their prayers rewarded more than the single individuals, and they will be following the path (Sunnah) of the Holy Prophet.

In reality, marriage is presented in Islamic teachings as much more than satisfying the intrinsic needs of human beings, but rather fulfilling the spiritual aspirations of humans in seeking the pleasure of Allah (swt). The Holy Prophet Mohammed (pbuh) is reported to have said:

"He who wishes to be cleaned and purified when he meets Allah should marry."

This holistic approach is intriguing, and should be an important factor in the minds of all, especially Muslims seeking to find a partner. The overall aim of our existence, as presented in the Holy Quran, is to seek perfection and righteousness through the worship of Allah (swt).

An important part of this realization is to work together, as husband and wife, in establishing a coherent and strong family based on the values and principles set out by our beautiful faith.

This brings immense rewards, both in this world and the next, and grants the couple a clearly defined goal to work towards. It would be prudent for the couple who have decided to commit themselves to marriage, and the responsibility that comes with it, to set the objective of seeking Paradise, while helping each other to get there.

A wonderful example of this commitment can be witnessed from the marriage of Imam Ali ibn Abi Talib (May Allah Bless Him) with the daughter of the Holy Prophet, Fatima (May Allah Bless Her). This family was a manifestation of the love of Allah (swt) and the service to others.

Traditions inform us of the self-sacrifice and altruism displayed by this household, resulting in a beautiful bond that remains a great example for all to follow. For instance, when Imam Ali (May Allah Bless Him) was asked about his wife Fatima, he replied:

'She is the best support in the fulfillment of the obedience of God.'

The Quran informs us (in 76:8) of how both Ali and Fatima sought to feed the orphans, the poor and the captives their food, whilst remaining hungry for three days. This could only happen if there is a common goal established amongst themselves.

Often, at the start of the journey of marriage, emphasis is placed on finding the right spouse, with the idea of 'compatibility' strongly in the minds of both men and women. Indeed, the religion of Islam does recommend that the foundation of faith and morality should be sought, as illustrated in the following tradition from the Holy Prophet Mohammed (pbuh):

"A man who marries a woman for the sake of her wealth, Allah leaves him in his own condition, and the one who marries her for her beauty, he will find in her (things) which he dislikes. But the one who marries a woman for the sake of her faith, Allah will gather all these things (beauty and wealth) for him." (Wasa'il Shia, v20, Bab 14: Hadith 14)

Finding harmony between husband and wife therefore requires common ground in many areas, including the moral, spiritual and intellectual fields. Based on this, both the male and female should ask important questions throughout this journey, such as: Why am I getting married? What do I want to achieve in marriage? What are my goals and aspirations in life? How do I achieve these aspirations?

In a world obsessed with outer appearances and presentations, Muslims must not forget to delve deeper, seeking that which reflects the purity of the soul and the softness of the heart.

Unfortunately we are living in societies where divorce rates are on the increase. In the United States, an estimated 40% of all marriages ended in divorce in

2008. Anecdotal evidence also suggests that the rise in divorce rates includes the Muslim communities. This should raise alarm bells, and highlight the need for careful consideration and thought by both parties before marriage.

A number of reasons have been cited for this rising trend. One involves the increasing expectations between couples that are often not met after marriage. This typically results in depression and loss of interest, leading to arguments and discord.

It's interesting to note that the Quran points to love and compassion building between the husband and wife after marriage, and not before:

"And of His signs is that He created for you mates from your own selves that you may take comfort in them, and He ordained affection and mercy between you. There are indeed signs in that for a people who reflect." Holy Quran (30:21)

This means that in order to establish a happy and fruitful marital relationship, both the husband and wife need to struggle together in understanding each other, overlooking faults and weaknesses, all the while building trust and love as their marriage progresses. This involves significant patience and perseverance, since problems and obstacles will invariably occur.

All this points to the importance of pre-marital preparation, the importance of equipping ourselves with the knowledge of what marriage entails, and understanding the differences that exist between men and women. The importance of effective communication cannot be over-emphasized, since too often, break downs in relationships are a result of poor communication between the husband and wife.

This book has been written to help the Muslim brothers and sisters understand how to initiate the journey of marriage. Rahat has done a great job in combining very useful advice with humorous anecdotes and examples, making the book an enjoyable read. I pray to The Almighty (swt) to reward him for his hard work, and to grant him success in both worlds.

Finally it is highly recommended, for those seeking to find the right partner in marriage, to recite verse (25:74) several times, sincerely asking for help from The Almighty and placing full trust in Him:

"And those who say, 'Our Lord! Give us joy and comfort in our spouses and offspring, and make us imams of the God-wary."

Mohammed Al-Hilli
The Holy City of Najaf
12 April 2014

# Chapter 1

# OVERVIEW

Despite the proliferation of the internet and new means of free and open communication, young adult Muslims find the process of finding someone to marry—and then actually marrying them—to be difficult and unwieldy.

The purpose of this book is to provide a guide to single, young adult Muslims on how to get married in a way that respects the rules and guidelines of Islam. At the same time, this book takes into consideration the realities of living in the modern era, particularly in a Western society.

Some entertaining stories are presented throughout the book showcasing interactions between various singles. Please take a moment to remember that Islam's teachings encourage a strong modicum of respect and a certain formal demeanor when interacting with individuals of the opposite gender. The stories are humorously presented without this aspect of Islamic behavior, and, accordingly, it is one of the reasons that each of these budding relationships does not work out.

Before educating and preparing you about intricacies of Western attitudes, this book will start with a bit of a warning on how awkward and sometimes embarrassing the process of getting married can be. This is not meant to scare you away; in fact, you will be given tips and strategies on how to reduce the chances of feeling awkward. If you do happen to feel embarrassed, the book will give you tips on how to calm tensions and move forward.

Then you will learn from a discussion on the importance of the marriage process and why you need to be involved in the decisions that relate to your own life. There will be reasoned and compelling arguments about why you should even want to be married and why it is important in your life, even if you currently feel otherwise. Don't worry—this book won't attempt to push you into marriage if you aren't ready, but it will give you food for thought.

Before you look for someone to marry, you should have a good idea of what you want to find (although, you should not have a strict list of criteria). Almost every person reading this book will immediately say, "I don't have any strict requirements, I just want a nice person with a good personality." While it is perfectly fine to say and think like that, it is important to realize that life is more nuanced and complex than finding a generically "nice" person and marrying them. You'll see how to think about what kind of person you want and get some guidance on how to avoid being too stringent before you even begin.

The next part of the book will deal with how you can prepare yourself for the process of finding someone to marry. Don't worry—it isn't that complicated, and with a few simple steps, you can be in an optimal state to begin the process.

After all that, there is not much else that can be done without actually coming into contact with a potential marriage candidate. This book will teach you how to appropriately meet someone you may be interested in and how to do so in a way that is more likely to be successful. To cover all your bases, this book will also feature a discussion on what to do if another individual has approached you and how you can respond in a way that preserves the respect and dignity of all parties involved. You will even learn how your response can probably help you get married or even avoid the wrong marital partner.

The process from here on out will be chock full of both direct and indirect cues. Learning about how to interpret indirect cues can make or break a potential marriage. This book will not delve into a never-ending discussion of hidden meanings for ordinary behavior but will attempt to teach you how to think about what actions you and the other party are taking, in context.

The question is often asked, "Now that I am talking to someone about marriage, what should I *actually* talk about?" And to be fair, this is a great question. Most people don't really know, and so they often get involved in conversations that are not relevant and can break apart a budding relationship with debates or arguments about unimportant topics. You'll see how you can avoid that and focus on conversation that helps you learn more about the other person and helps you reach a decision about what you want to do in terms of marriage.

There's "talking" and then there is "the conversation." At some point, you and the other individual will need to speak to each other directly about whether to take the process to the next level (usually getting engaged) or to halt the process because it is not working. Until and unless you have this conversation, you will never, ever, get married (unless your parents are going to have "the conversation" with the other person's parents themselves). This conversation is called the DTR which stands for "determine the relationship." This will be covered in depth and will provide you with the tools you need to have to get through the conversation.

If you move forward after the DTR, you will need to involve your parents and so will the other individual. This is the second scariest part of getting married, so you'll need to review the chapter on how to successfully navigate the conversation with your parents.

In the twenty-first century, it's often the case that parents know as much about the process as you do (close to nothing) and will need your guidance on what to do next, how to contact the other parents, what to say to them, and how to have conversations in general. The more you can be in control of this process, the better off you will be.

Once the parents agree to the marriage, there will be a series of stressful, awkward, and completely important negotiations that they will engage in. One chapter will discuss some of the nuances of that process and how to navigate those (sometimes scary) waters.

After this point, things become progressively easier and harder at the same time. The most exciting part of the next few months, for many, will be telling everyone you know about your impending marriage.

This book will not give you any advice on how to plan a wedding or what it should be like, but it will direct you towards books that can help you plan your marriage itself and how to plan for a lifetime of happiness.

After having read this guide, it is likely that you will be on much steadier footing in your attempts to get married. Good luck and have fun!

# Chapter 2

# WELL THIS IS
# AWKWARD ...

The first aspect that must be learned and engrained into your mind is that this entire process, from the first day you begin, until approximately a year after you become married, is going to be awkward.

This is a reality that is present in not only Muslim culture but in every society and group of people in the world. Awkwardness has been a part of the marriage process for the entire history of time and probably enduring on forever into the future.

The awkwardness of this process comes from the fact that there will always be some degree of embarrassment at each step that progressively leads to a marriage. Whether it is the first time you speak to a potential marriage partner or the first time you speak to his or her parents, or most moments in between or after, you will feel awkward.

The reason for this feeling is that new situations tend to make people feel self-conscious. This is because at each successive step, increasingly private aspects of your life will be revealed to your potential marriage partner and to his or her family.

Details of your educational and professional history will be discussed openly and, oftentimes, in dissecting detail. Your ability to be either a providing husband or a nurturing wife will be analyzed in open conversation by both your family and the family of your potential marital partner.

While sometimes embarrassing, it is a necessary aspect of bringing someone into a permanent position in your life. The only fact that may alleviate these feelings is the truth that it also will be happening to whomever you choose to marry, at the same time, by the same people.

Of course, that is much further down the line. At the beginning, the person that will most stringently analyze you and be your biggest critic, pointing out your major and minor flaws and exaggerating your inadvertent behavior, will be you.

The most common thoughts you will have are, "Am I doing this correctly?" followed by, "Are they going to laugh at me or be mad at me if I do this wrong?" There are many different ways these thoughts and feelings are described. Common phrases that describe the same experience include feeling weird, uncomfortable, tongue-tied, self-conscious, uneasy, out of your depth, and simply embarrassed.

Invariably, there are some people who take this to an extreme. These people are so off-put by the awkward feelings that they prematurely stop discussions with possible marriage partners.

What happens is that such people start assuming that the other party is to blame or that there really isn't the realistic possibility of a match between the two because of these feelings, or they manage to come up with a few other excuses.

Some people become so infatuated with the idea of avoiding awkward scenarios and feelings that they delay marriage for many years, often to their own detriment.

To be fair, sometimes a situation is more awkward than normal, and it actually *is* because of the other person. In these situations, it's best to try to alleviate the problem and see if the interaction can be salvaged.

Something that is important to think about is, "Should I judge someone as a potential partner in marriage when they are simply having a bad day?"

Everyone has a bad day once in a while, including

you. It usually a good idea to try to find out if the other person is simply having bad luck or not feeling well or if there really is a conflict of personalities.

The best way to find out if you are compatible with another person is to try to understand the perspectives of potential marriage partners and their families.

In doing so, you will be able to make a more realistic assessment of whether you actually want to get married to a particular person.

Sometimes the conclusion will be that you should not marry this person, and that's perfectly fine—if it is for the right reasons, which we will discuss later on in this book.

*     *     *

Recently, at one of the annual conventions where large numbers of Muslims attend, Zeeshan was present at the convention's matrimonial event—these events have become popular and commonplace.

At the event, he met a young sister named Rizwana whom he became interested in speaking with.

He thought about asking to meet with her but wasn't sure how to do it or how to meet with her.

"What if she thinks I'm not religious because I want

to meet with her instead of attending the lectures?" he thought.

"But, what if she thinks I don't really like her because I would rather attend the lectures instead of meet with her?" Zeeshan conversely pondered.

Rizwana noticed that Zeeshan seemed to be quite nervous when he was around her. Finally, Zeeshan asked her to meet with him at a coffee shop near the convention hall. Rizwana spoke with her parents, and they agreed that she would be allowed to go.

Rizwana was looking forward to the meeting, as Zeeshan seemed to be a very nice individual and polite with her family as well.

However, when Zeeshan got to the coffee shop and sat down with Rizwana, he let his nerves overwhelm him. The same nervous thoughts he had before asking to meet with Rizwana seemed to dominate conversation.

"Do you think I should be missing this lecture?" was one of the first things Zeeshan asked Rizwana, worried that she would think he wasn't religious.

"I'm not sure what you mean?" Rizwana replied, not understanding why Zeeshan would bring this up.

"Oh, I just want you to understand that I value this

meeting highly, that's why I'm missing the lecture."

"Oh ok ... So tell me about yourself. What is your profession?" Rizwana wanted to bring the conversation back on track.

"Well, I've been working at the same company for a few years. I manage a team. What about you?"

Rizwana smiled. It seemed that they could start getting to know one another, "Well, actually I –"

Zeeshan interrupted, "You are sure it is okay that I'm missing the lecture, right?"

Rizwana's smile fell.

"Uh, yea?"

"Good ... good, I'm just making sure. I'm not the kind of person that skips lectures you know. I try to be as religious as possible."

"Oh ... well, I don't want you do to anything you aren't comfortable with." Rizwana paused as she continued, "If this lecture is that important to you, I don't want to keep you from it, but we are already here ..."

Starting to sweat, Zeeshan nodded. "Great, I guess we'll have to meet later! I'll see you at the conference."

With that, Zeeshan quickly left the coffee shop and went back to the convention, leaving Rizwana sitting alone in the café with two cups of coffee in front of her, both still steaming hot.

*     *     *

Zeeshan knew he blew it. He really liked Rizwana, but the fact of the matter was, he couldn't get over his nervous thoughts, and even though Rizwana seemed to be okay with his anxiousness, he let his feelings overwhelm him.

Unfortunately, awkward feelings and behavior are simply an aspect of the process that cannot be avoided. However, this does not mean that there's nothing you can do.

Understanding that a situation is awkward can help you overcome it. Oftentimes the solution is as simple as taking a deep breath, clearing your mind, and moving on from any mistakes or errors.

It is typical that you, the person you are meeting with, or someone else nearby will make a comment that is awkward, embarrassing, or unintelligent in some way or another.

If it is the person you are meeting with, or anyone else, the best course of action is to smile and change the topic of conversation. Everyone feels nervous, and the opportunity to display empathy will help you earn the respect of others.

Dwelling on a topic that seems to make the other person nervous does not help you make a decision about that person. Meeting someone in a situation that is slightly awkward, where that person is not as comfortable as they would usually be, does not give the most accurate representation of who that person is.

It is often the case that once the awkwardness has subsided, you will find that the perhaps clumsy or shy person you began conversation with is actually a warm and caring person. In most situations, once the awkwardness subsides, you may notice the true character of the person in both positive and negative ways. It is to your own advantage to make the person you are speaking with as comfortable as possible so that you can see who they really are and whether they are worth moving forward with.

It is virtually a guarantee that you will make a comment, or do something else, that will make you feel immediately embarrassed or awkward. Hopefully, it is not something that is truly offensive and was accidental in nature. Regardless of what you do or what happens, the way to overcome the situation is clear and simple.

Just move on. Don't be afraid to laugh at yourself or feel a bit embarrassed. These things are normal, and it is very likely that the other person will realize it.

If you have accidently said or done something that is offensive, immediately apologize. "I'm sorry, I did not mean that" or "My apologies—that was wrong of me to say" are examples of how to respectfully acknowledge your mistake.

Then, as before, simply move on to a new topic of conversation. The topic of conversation doesn't matter, but the display of social awareness that you exercise in being able to recover from an embarrassing, awkward, or bad situation will demonstrate maturity and depth of character.

It is important that you do not dwell on what has happened or attempt to launch into lengthy explanations of what you meant, unless it comes up organically in the course of conversation. This will only cause you to become unnecessarily nervous and will make the conversation even more awkward. If it does come up naturally in conversation, do not feel worried or be afraid. Calmly discuss the topic in a confident and relaxed manner.

It is important for you to realize that throughout the

process of finding a partner in marriage, the individuals you meet with are not interested in judging you or "getting rid" of you for the slightest infraction. They are speaking with you for only one reason—to understand if you are a good match for them. It is the exact same reason why you are speaking to them.

Finally, the last lesson this chapter contains is that whatever your feelings are, no matter how awkward, nervous, or embarrassed you feel, you will get through it. As mentioned earlier, awkwardness in this process is a part of every culture, every period of history, and will always be there for generations to come. Despite this fact, countless individuals have gotten past the initial stages and lived happily ever after. The same will be true for you, *inshallah*, so don't worry, and let's move on to the next chapter.

# Chapter 3

# WHY SHOULD I CARE ABOUT GETTING MARRIED?

*I'm too young to be thinking about this.*

*I'm not ready to get married.*

*I've got to find myself first.*

*I'm not really interested in marriage right now.*

*I'll let my parents take care of that when they want to.*

These are some of the excuses that many young adult Muslims provide when asked about marriage. In some cases, it is true that an individual is too young to get married or is not ready to get married in terms of education or career, but barring those circumstances (discussed in the next chapter), marriage is more than appropriate for everyone.

Islam strongly recommends marriage for all Muslim men and women. There are no exceptions to this recommendation, and Islam rejects the idea that individuals can be more religious, pious, or adherent to belief without first becoming married.

The Holy Prophet (SAW) of Islam says, "One who has become married has completed half of his [or her] *deen*." This statement means that an individual who has become married has completed a major requirement for those seeking to follow Islam. The act of marriage is so important that it literally equals "half of the belief of Islam. "

This is a bit of an awkward statement in the English language, as the phrase 'half of *deen*' is difficult to translate in such a way as to convey the true meaning.

To more appropriately understand this phrase, it may be more correct to say that it means that an individual completes a great majority of the expectations of Allah when they become married—fifty percent of these expectations in fact.

The Prophet continues by stating that the sleep of a married individual is worth more than the night-long prayers of an unmarried person. To put that into context, the average night is approximately eight to ten hours, and a healthy adult could likely perform literally hundreds of *rakaats* of *mustaheb,* or recommended, prayers in that time frame.

Yet, no matter how much an unmarried person could pray in this time, the married person obtains more reward merely by going to sleep.

There is not any particular miracle associated with a married person's sleep. The extra reward is due to the fact that the sleep of the married person enables them to be rested and prepared for the next day of marriage, and Islam values a strong and healthy marriage. Every act that supports and solidifies a marriage is worthy of reward in the teachings of Islam, and so even the minor act of sleep merits divine blessings.

*   *   *

There are practical reasons for marriage as well. Whether you consider yourself to be an introvert or an extrovert or a 'loner' or any other self-descriptive term you may choose to utilize, human beings require interaction with other people.

A recent study shows that shy people get married just as often as outgoing individuals. This means there is someone for everyone.

Interacting with other people, whether they are friends, family, or colleagues, dictates how the majority of your time is spent, especially so in the twenty-first century and in the Western world. It is an inescapable fact of life, and it is a truth that you should utilize for your advantage.

Unless you plan to live your life in solitude, on a mountain or in some faraway place, you will always interact with others. However, the people you interact with, besides your family members, will come into your life and leave your life based upon their own life choices and goals.

Your friends will get into schools, get jobs, get married, have kids, move away, become busy, change personalities, and engage in all sorts of regular life experiences that will have nothing to do with you.

It will not be because they are upset with you or because they do not want to be friends with you, it is simply a fact that everyone must live their own lives.

Your closest friends will likely speak with you about their plans that will likely take them out of your life and may even involve you in the decision-making process.

In rare circumstances, you will actually have friends that stay local and have time to be as close as they ever were until you both become old and grey. However, the vast majority of your friends, even your close ones, will eventually live their lives in a way that is best for them.

Over time, you will make friends and lose friends, repeatedly, and the problem is that there will not be any consistent person in your life. There will not be a person who really knows you, for your whole life, except for your own family members.

The major exception to this list is your spouse.

Loneliness is a major aspect of the modern era and Western life. Despite cell phones, Facebook, and instant messaging, it is a reality that the majority of young adults, especially Muslims, feel a major sense of loneliness. Young Muslims attempt to fill the void of loneliness with a variety of activities and practices.

Some people listen to music, for hours every single day, simply to avoid feeling alone. While for some, this works temporarily, as the lyrics appear to drown out thoughts of loneliness, it never works permanently.

As soon as the music stops, the feelings return, and the cycle continues anew. For some, the music isn't helpful even in the slightest, as listening to music means that one is not engaging in conversation. With conversation literally nonexistent, it is hard to avert the feelings of loneliness that surface.

Others obsessively turn to social media, attempting to utilize Facebook, Twitter, GroupMe, WhatsApp,

Snapchat, Vine, and countless other social networks to interact with other people as much as possible.

There's nothing wrong with social media if used properly, however, the purpose of social media is not to completely or majorly fulfill your need for human interaction. Because of this truth, it never satisfies users sufficiently to make them feel less lonely.

Still others attempt to interact with new and old friends, of both genders, believing that loneliness can be resolved through any type of platonic social contact. While this method involves face-to-face dialogue and interaction, it only works for a short time. Seeing your friends every few days helps to avert some loneliness, but outside of college, this is extremely difficult. For working professionals, it is arduous to see friends more than once or twice a week. As you grow older, a more realistic number sometimes becomes "every few weeks."

Even if you see friends as often as you desire, the reality is that everyone is created with the need for companionship in the way of marriage.

Regardless of how often you see your friends or how many friends you have, the role that friends play in your life will vary.

While for some, the right friends can take away some

loneliness, over time, these same friends become involved in their own lives, and that can take up much of their energy and focus.

You should have friends, and you should not feel that you have to give up social media if you are using it appropriately. You should also not feel lonely, and you should not feel the need to go searching for ways to temporarily stave off loneliness.

What you should have is a true partner in marriage who understands and knows you, who is there for you and supports you, who stands with you in adversity, and stands behind you when you need to be pushed in life.

You should have a spouse that is always "in your corner" in a way that no one else will be. A partner who is all these things, and more, for the rest of your life.

That is why you should get married—because nothing else can truly compare.

*     *     *

As important and as useful as it is to get married, it is imperative that the process of meeting a partner in marriage be taken seriously. The reputations of many people will be directly affected by your actions.

The comments and decisions you make will dictate how people think of you and your family and could have strong effects on anyone you choose to consider for the sake of marriage.

If your goal is to simply meet someone and have fun with someone of the opposite gender, then you should pause and reflect upon your goals.

Whatever this book advises should never be taken as recommending or allowing for mere dating. There is no provision in Islam for dating amongst single individuals, no matter how it is defined, in any context.

The marriage process that is allowed by Islam is best described as a research, emotional analysis, and interview process wherein you will make a lifelong decision that will create a relationship between you and another individual.

Emotions will play a major role in whatever actions you take. Words such as honor, love, compatibility, respect, dignity, and consideration for others will be key parts of your thoughts throughout this process.

You will be well served by respecting that both others and you will feel strong emotions throughout the process and that it is important to respect the feelings of others as much as possible.

\*   \*   \*

"Abid, where are you?" Abid's mother called to him.

"I'm here," Abid replied from the kitchen, "Just getting a snack."

"A snack?" she replied, confused. "I thought you went to dinner."

Sheepishly Abid responded, "Yes, I did, I'm just still a bit hungry."

His mother frowned. Abid typically did not like to eat again after dinner, as he was very health-conscious.

"How was dinner with Aleena? I was speaking with her mother while you were both out, and we are very excited. Hopefully this will be a great match for our families."

Abid did not reply, quietly staring at the food in the refrigerator.

"Abid, what is it? Did you not like her? Don't be worried if she was shy—lots of good girls are shy and don't like to talk at these first meetings."

"No … it wasn't that, I think we just aren't the same type of personality."

"Oh my son, you know that I love you very much,

but I am very close with Aleena's mother, Humaira Aunty. How can I just say that there were different personalities? Maybe you can talk to her on the phone a little bit and see her one more time."

"I'm not sure that's going to help."

"Abid, I'm your mother. Trust me! I know these things. After you both get comfortable, then everything will be better."

"Mom … it's just not going to work out."

Abid was not the type to resist so strongly without a good reason. Abid's mother began to realize that something unusual had happened.

"Okay, then you are going to have to tell me what really happened." She ushered Abid to the kitchen table. "Come come, I'll heat some food for you."

Abid sat at the table, his eyes still not meeting his mother's gaze.

"Abid, tell me about the dinner."

"It's nothing Mom …"

"Right now Abid, tell me."

Abid sighed. Resigned to having to tell the story, he began.

"Well, I got to the restaurant about five minutes early, but Aleena was about forty-five minutes late."

"Well, that's a bit late even for our standards," his mother responded, referring to her community's tendency to be late to most events "… But sometimes it's okay. I hope that's not the reason you don't want to see her again."

"No, I was fine with that, but she brought someone with her when she arrived."

"Oh Abid, we discussed this. Either her brother or her cousin was going to be there to be like a chaperone."

"Well I know that, but this guy wasn't her relative. His name was Trevor, and they sat very close to each other on the other side of the booth."

His mother's eyes widened.

"Aleena told me she wasn't hungry. She had just gotten dinner with Trevor—that's why she was so late. Trevor left, and I thought perhaps the evening could be salvaged, but it just got worse. She just kept talking about how nice Trevor was and how grateful she was to have a friend like him. Any time I tried to talk to her about her hobbies or tell her about mine, she would switch the conversation to Trevor's hobbies and his interests."

Abid's mother felt embarrassed—she knew that it was hard for her son to be admitting how awful the night went.

"I lost my appetite quickly. After a while of that, I had enough. I was polite and thanked her for her time, but then I left."

"Maybe you are right, Abid. I had no idea she was like that."

"Mom …"

"Yes Abid? What is it?"

"You've known Humaira Aunty for fifteen years. I don't think she knows Aleena is like this at all, and I don't think she would respond well if she found out."

Abid paused and took a deep breath.

"So what are you going to say to her?"

\*     \*     \*

It is clear that Aleena was not interested in Abid, for one reason or another. However, instead of being direct with Abid about her feelings and decisions, she behaved in such a way that caused Abid, Abid's mother, and her own mother, Humaira, to all become involved in an uncomfortable situation.

More likely than not, the fifteen-year friendship between the two mothers might be irreparably damaged, simply because Aleena did not want to behave in a respectful manner.

The best advice is advice that you have already heard before: Treat others just as you would wish to be treated. Treat others just as you would want your own brother, sister, son, or daughter to be treated.

If you take this advice, and the individuals you consider for marriage follow it too, the process of finding a spouse will be one of the most pleasant and memorable experiences of your lifetime.

Finding your opportunity to live happily ever after is as simple as treating others with respect until you find the right person to marry.

# Chapter 4

# WHEN TO GET MARRIED

Before we continue, it is worth discussing age ranges for those who are starting to think about marriage. This is a short chapter, because there really is not very much to say about it. Each person's circumstance involves details that are particular and unique, especially for people in younger age ranges. You will have to make the decision for yourself, depending on the circumstances of your life and the logistics of your family situation.

If you are a freshman or sophomore in college or younger, this book cannot offer any advice to you regarding marriage timing, as such discussions are best had with your family.

*   *   *

Farhan adjusted his tie.

"I'm still in school. I'd like to be an engineer someday," he told the sisters at the table.

He was seated with three other brothers and four sisters at a matrimonial convention for Muslims. The brothers were all wearing suits, and the sisters were similarly dressed in an elegant fashion.

Across the table, Yasmina asked, "Oh that's great, what kind of engineer would you like to be?"

"I'm not exactly sure," Farhan replied easily. "I have a few years to figure it out."

The others at the table looked him.

"I thought you said you were a junior—don't you graduate next year?" a brother seated to his right named Akber asked.

"I will, from Fairfield High School. I'm starting to look at some great colleges. I hope I can get a scholarship!"

Stunned, the other participants at the table looked at one another.

"Bro, this convention is for serious participants only. We all are here to find a husband or a wife. Do you seriously want to get married at your age?" Akber demanded of Farhan.

"No, of course not. I'm way too young."

Yasmina spoke up—the whole situation was just too weird. "Then what are you doing here?"

Farhan adjusted his tie again, leaned back in his chair, and smiled.

"Just practicing."

*   *   *

Some individuals truly are too young to get married. Depending upon your local laws, it might not even be legal for you to get married. If you are in early college, or are younger than that, please behave responsibly.

The process of getting married is a very serious endeavor and, in the case of younger individuals, must be discussed with your family before proceeding. Don't be in a rush to get married before you are ready for it.

For those who are the appropriate age to get married, there is a gender disparity in age ranges in the marital progress. This is a fact of Muslim culture and will continue to be the case for the foreseeable future. The disparity is that it is acceptable for Muslim women to become married at a slightly younger age than would be the case for Muslim men.

Of course, this does not speak to the teachings of Islam which provides no such disparity and is entirely neutral in this regard. The noticed disparity is not one that is "recommended" but is merely an observation of how culture functions in the modern era and in the Western world.

Indeed, this particular cultural attitude is likely also true in the Middle East and African and South Asian Muslim communities as well.

It is somewhat common for marriages to take place where the husband is working in his chosen profession while the wife is somewhat younger and may even be a junior or senior in college.

Generally, for both genders, if you are someone who has graduated college and are either working or engaged in graduate studies, you are old enough to get married.

It is strongly advised to not delay marriage. It is a fact of reality that for both genders it is increasingly difficult to find a suitable marriage partner as you grow older. This is due to the fact that if a person is a worthy single, another individual will quickly discover this and pursue marriage with them.

There are 1.2 billion Muslims in the world, but only a fraction of them are in your community, and only a small percentage of them are in age ranges that you would consider. The majority of people that would be called a "great catch" will get married at an early age.

It is not impossible to find an excellent match when you are outside of what your community considers the "prime" age to marry, but to find such a match will require significantly more effort than if you were younger.

For some people, the last two chapters were not necessary, as they are ready and excited to look for a partner in marriage, but for those who weren't, *inshallah*, everyone is on the same page now. In the next chapter, we'll discuss exactly what kind of person you should be looking for. We will discuss issues related to character, background, personality, and a plethora of other considerations to watch for.

# Chapter 5

# AVOIDING THE TRAP OF USING THE WRONG JUDGMENT CRITERIA

Tall. Light-colored skin. Syed. From a good family. Doctor.

To be fair, this is likely not your actual list of characteristics that you think about or desire for your partner in marriage. It may be a list that is imposed on you from a cultural perspective or from certain members of your friends or family.

The problem with this oft-repeated list of characteristics is that literally none of those descriptors have anything to do with a happy, successful, Islamic marriage. The entire list doesn't even contain an adjective that actually describes a person to any degree whatsoever.

Imagine if this sort of list was how you as an individual were defined. Instead of characteristics such as your personality, your interests, your life experiences, you were relegated to a two- or three-word description that related only to your height or skin tone.

While this probably isn't your list, it is important to full understand why it should never be anyone's list.

Physical characteristics do matter, but you must ask yourself how much they should matter in your final decision. Put another way, for each individual, looks and appearance matter in some way or another, and that is natural and acceptable.

Although appearance may be an important consideration, it is recommended that it not be the first consideration and especially not be the most important consideration. While most people realize this, you may not realize that you are inadvertently placing a much stronger emphasis on appearance than is warranted.

*     *     *

Nasreen stepped into the matrimonial convention hall. It was her first time attending one of these events, and she was not sure what to expect. Rahela, her best friend, had just gotten married from a match she met at one of these events and recommended the process to her.

*Why not give it a shot?* thought Nasreen.

As she stepped in, the first thing she noticed was how many people were in the room. The room was packed with young professional Muslims of both genders. As Nasreen stepped through the door, she was followed by several others, eager to register for the program.

Soon, her optimism faded. She examined the room.

*No one really looks that interesting today.*

*This might have been good for Rahela, but everyone's different,* Nasreen thought. *Maybe I got a bad batch …*

A voice interrupted her thoughts.

"As Salaam Alaikum sister, my name is Yusuf. Would you like to sign in?"

*Ah, a volunteer.*

She made her decision.

"Sorry brother, I was just leaving."

\*     \*     \*

Nasreen may not realize it, but all that she has done is look at a room of people full of potential candidates, observed their appearance for a few moments, perhaps less than a minute, and then dismissed an entire group of people without having any knowledge about their personalities, compatible aspects, or any personal characteristics. Unfortunately, she took the most superficial aspect about a group of people and used that information to make a major life decision to reject each person.

You probably don't think it's a big deal, but here's the twist: Someone has done that to you. You've been in a room, maybe at a wedding, perhaps at a convention, or even at a party. You were well-well dressed and happily interacting with the other attendees.

You may not have noticed, but someone walked into that room and made a decision that you, and every single person around you, was not attractive enough to even consider for more than a few seconds.

This decision was made without hearing your voice— without considering what kind of person you are, your personality, ethics, morality, humor, warmth, or any other characteristic that you value about yourself.

The decision was made without knowing about your interests or hobbies, your educational or professional accomplishments, without hearing about your devotion to Islam and community service.

Instead it was made based upon what you happened to be wearing and other irrelevant aspects, such as the lighting, the social environment, and the persons standing around you.

This idea that you were ignored and rejected in this way doesn't feel good does it?

Another question: Did the person who rejected you, without even meeting you, make a decision that was well-reasoned, that considered the relevant factors, and that will make them happier in the long run?

Of course not! And they probably missed out on a great opportunity to get to know you.

If you, or anyone else, behave this way, you are ratcheting up the importance of appearance to 100% of your consideration and every other factor down to zero percent. *Inshallah*, you will be married for the rest of your life, and, as such, it is vital that you get to know the personality, character, and morals of the other person before you commit to marriage.

\*    \*    \*

In some cultures and in particular families, great and overwhelming focus is placed on the notion that Syeds (descendants of the Holy Prophet) must, and may only, marry other Syeds. This is an ideology that is rejected by all sects and branches of Islam.

Indeed, when examining the life of the Holy Prophet and looking at his family and descendants from the

Ahlul Bayt (the original Syeds), only approximately a very small percentage of his family members, for the proceeding twelve generations, married other Syeds at all. From amongst the Imams of the Ahlul Bayt, only two have married Syeds.

Today, scholars of both the Shia and Sunni schools of thought have unanimously dismissed the idea that it is either recommended or mandatory for Syeds to marry one another.

The Al Azhar Seminary in Egypt, the top theological institute in the four Sunni schools of thought (*madhab*), has given no credence to the notion that it is preferable for Syeds to marry one another.

Similarly, every Grand Ayatollah in the Shia school of *fiqh* has clearly articulated that while it is, of course, allowed for Syeds to marry one another, there is no special requirement to do so, nor is there any particular benefit in doing so.

Further clarifying the issue, they have indicated the same holds true regardless of whether it is a male Syed or female Syed seeking to marry a non-Syed.

\*    \*    \*

Education is a vital component in examining any potential marriage candidate, although, like any other characteristic, it should not be the only aspect that you look for. Education plays a vital role in determining many aspects about the future marriage.

For example, the amount of education and manner in which it was done will give strong insights into the profession of the person you are considering and about possibilities for advancement.

Certainly it is advisable to make every effort to understand the nature of the education that the other person has pursued (or is currently pursuing).

For example, there are many different types of engineers, lawyers, medical doctors, researchers, and IT professionals. In fact, there probably multiple career paths in any given profession, many of which can be dictated by education.

Any attempt you make to learn more about the degree your potential marriage candidate is pursuing will help you to understand what your future may hold if you go through with marriage with this particular individual.

Careful consideration must be given to ensure that you do not search for only one type of profession in your marriage partner.

It is quite common in many Muslim cultures that

singles are encouraged to seek out and marry medical doctors, above all other professions, as a primary goal.

While it is true that medical doctors enjoy many financial benefits and are highly regarded in the Muslim community, a strategy of ignoring all candidates except for medical doctors is unwise.

First, the most practical consideration is that having a medical degree does not give any information as to what kind of person an individual is. It gives no clues to their personality, ability to function in a marriage, warmth of character, or religious values. Doctors, like anyone else, have differing personalities and are not all exactly the same as one another.

Next, it is a reality that only a small percentage of the Muslim community are doctors. Choosing a strategy of only considering medical doctors means that you are eliminating more than ninety percent of candidates, without any practical benefit to yourself.

In modern society, it is clear that finding the right marriage partner is both very important and not easy. Accordingly, reducing the number of possible candidates does not help you and may, in fact, cause you to miss out on great opportunities.

Finally, there are a multitude of career paths and professions that provide equivalent or superior stability to that of medical doctors. There is nothing wrong with marrying a doctor, and there is nothing wrong with marrying an individual that has any *halal* career path.

There is something wrong with marrying someone exclusively because of their career or rejecting a candidate simply because of their career. You will find that no single aspect of any individual will immediately and definitively lead to the kind of marriage you have always wanted, but a combination of the right factors will do so.

\* \* \*

"Medicine is important," said Khuram to his friend Jaleel. "Someone has got to do it."

The two were enjoying lunch together, having another one of their deep conversations.

"Yea, but why place so much importance on it as a career?" Jaleel responded.

"Well how else am I supposed to get married and be happy Jay?" Khuram retorted, using an old nickname for his childhood friend.

"Khuram, I do understand—I've heard you say it a thousand times. Doctors provide financial stability, they work hard, and they are caring people."

"Then why are we having this discussion again Jay?" Khuram sighed.

"It's just weird man," Jaleel replied, starting to become agitated.

"It's not weird at all Jaleel."

With a practiced deliberation, Khuram took a bite of his pizza and then washed it down with soda.

He spoke up again.

"I've said it once and I'll say it again: I'm going to find a doctor to marry so she can take care of me financially. If she is a nice person, that's just icing on the cake. You know, it's a great plan. You should try it too! We can be stay-at-home husbands."

Not sure how to react, Jaleel simply shook his head and wondered how it all went so wrong.

\* \* \*

As stated, education is important, and you must take it into consideration, however, like any other factor, it is only one piece of the pie and should not be a criterion to eliminate otherwise worthwhile candidates. Please take this advice to heart, and continue your search with an open mind and an open heart. A successful and happy marriage has many factors; career and education are only some of the calculation.

# Chapter 6

# SOUL MATES AND
# SOUL TRAITS

Finding your soul mate can be hard. Especially, because in Islam, *there is no concept of a soul mate*. Even more so because the concept of a soul mate does not exist in any religion, philosophy, or belief system around the world, except in Hollywood.

The concept of a soul mate is found nowhere in the books of Judaism, Christianity, Islam, Buddhism, Hinduism, or any other holy text.

The entire concept was fabricated for the purposes of TV and movies. Yes, that's right—the idea of a soul mate is as real as Batman.

But that does not mean that you can't find your perfect match. The difficulty in understanding this concept can be clarified by understanding what a "soul mate" has been portrayed to be and what logic, reason, and Islam tell us we should look for.

A soul mate, according to various forms of romance

literature and movies, is an individual with whom you are "destined" to be. This person was chosen to be your "one true love" before you were born, and every relationship you attempt to form with anyone else will be a failure. You have no control over who this person is or when you will encounter them. Nor do you have any idea who they are. You can only guess if the person you are married to is your soul mate, because no one can ever truly confirm it for you.

Frankly, it doesn't really sound all that great, because it is an idea that espouses that you do not have any control over your life, and you should not even try to find a marriage partner because no matter what you do or don't do, you will end up with them anyways.

You wouldn't believe this kind of setup in any other scenario. For example, if you were told that you were destined to get an A+ on an exam, no matter how little you studied, you wouldn't believe it, would you?

If your car had engine problems, you wouldn't believe that it would get fixed on its own. You wouldn't believe that "destiny" would fix your car issues, even if you avoided mechanics and car repair shops.

Nor would you believe that you would get the perfect career without any effort.

Actually, you would never believe anyone who told

you that you would get any major change in life without smart planning, dedicated efforts, and your sincere intentions.

Finding the best match, however, is entirely possible, and it is entirely up to you if you want to marry someone who is your perfect match.

To be clear, no one you will encounter for marriage is perfect. Frankly, you are not perfect either. No one individual will ever satisfy every single preconception you have, and it is important to realize that at an early stage. You should not be looking for someone to fit a list of pre-determined criteria; you should be looking for someone who is your match.

What or who is your perfect match? It is someone with whom you can work together to build a strong, religious, and happy marriage.

That sentence probably caused you to pause and say, "What?" The only words in your mind right now are probably "work together"?

You are probably thinking that using that particular phrase is quite cold and clinical and does not describe any sort of ideal marriage. However, nothing could be further from the truth.

You have always realized you wanted such a person,

but you probably used different words to describe the same idea. It is likely that you have always wanted someone you "got along with."

In fact, both phrases portray the exact same idea, except "work together" gives a little bit more specificity as to what you actually should want.

Working with your spouse means that whatever future you want for yourself and your family, you can discuss it with your husband or wife and make a plan to ensure that it comes to light.

It means proactively pursuing happiness and comfort in life instead of passively hoping that everything works out. Working together with your spouse also means using your logic and intellect to pursue happiness.

To expand the analogy of "working together," look at your office environment. The people you best work together with are most likely to be your friends. The person you like working with most is probably a nice, fun person who you maintain a social friendship with.

The same should be true of how you perceive your spouse. They should be your close friend with whom you accomplish important goals. In the case of marriage, the goals are not for a business purpose, they are for the purpose of giving you both a feeling of long-term happiness.

However, sometimes, there is more than pure logic that makes a successful marriage.

Another specific aspect of getting along with another individual is the notion of a type of "intangible compatibility." This is best described as the easy and comfortable manner of discourse that sometimes becomes apparent when speaking with another person for the sake of marriage.

In another sense, Hollywood and Western cultures may refer to this same concept as "chemistry," although there are key differences.

In television and movies, chemistry refers to physical attraction without reasoned thought. This type of chemistry is inherently rejected by Islam and does not help anyone select a compatible partner.

A person may be attractive in a particular way but have an incompatible or poor personality. Of course the opposite may be true, but you will never be able to ascertain this simply by looking at them.

There is a limit to the type of interactions that males and females may have before marriage, and, in most cases, initial and exploratory conversations with marriage candidates are generally deemed permissible.

For details on further limits, it is best advised that you consult a trustworthy and knowledgeable Islamic scholar.

Chemistry, in the context of an Islamic relationship, is the ability to engage in easy, free-flowing conversation without the feeling of trepidation. Put another way, you will find that conversation comes naturally with the other person and that you do not struggle to find topics of conversation.

That you have a modicum of comfort with someone, or "chemistry," may present itself in various ways. Perhaps you will find that you have similar viewpoints on a variety of topics, similar interests, or you might be amused to find that you dislike similar things.

No list is comprehensive and no list is dispositive and each person will find that "chemistry" will display itself in different ways particular to your personality.

*   *   *

An aspect that is tangible, and is sometimes (but not always) apparent on your first meeting with a potential marriage candidate, is *character*.

The ethics, integrity, honor, dignity, or morality of an individual are important to examine and should be of the utmost concern. Indeed, this aspect will influence your marriage more than any other factor.

How can you ascertain a person's character? In fact, there are several ways, and it's best to try them all. The most straightforward method is to simply ask your potential marriage candidate direct questions about issues relating to morality and its role in your possible future marriage.

*How do you think the concept of morality applies in marriage?*

*What are your most important ethical values?*

*Can integrity be taught to our hypothetical future children and, if so, how?*

These are just a few examples of the types of questions to ask; presumably you will need to come up with your own list.

As much as conversation can tell you, direct observation of behavior will tell you at least as much, if not more. Please be warned, this story showcases some of the inappropriate informality that Islam advises against.

\*   \*   \*

Laughing, Kameela took another sip of her water. Mansoor could clearly see that Kameela was a very nice, happy, and well-rounded person. Her light natured and fun personality was very evident.

"Miss, I'm sorry, could I get several slices of lemon, like six or seven?"

The waitress nodded and walked away to pick up the order.

Mansoor thought this was odd, *Lemon doesn't really go with pizza …*

"Anyways, Mansoor, as I was saying, doing the right thing is the most important virtue to me. I really believe that as Muslims we have a responsibility to behave with the best possible *akhlaaq*. If we show that we are good moral people, then relations with non-Muslims will get better."

The waitress returned with the lemon slices, and Kameela graciously thanked her.

When she left, she lowered her voice to a whisper and said, "I love lemonade, but I hate paying three dollars for it. So I just get these free lemon wedges, mix in some sugar, and I am in great shape!"

Mansoor raised his eyebrows in surprise.

"… Really?"

"Oh yea, it's perfect. It's like totally funny. Anyways, like I was saying, it is really important that we portray the best image about ourselves. You never know who could be watching, so we always need to be on our best behavior."

Kameela took another sip of her lemonade.

"Yea, I guess you really don't realize who might be paying attention to your actions," Mansoor responded. He was still having a hard time understanding the free lemonade but mentally brushed it aside for now.

"So tell me Kameela, I heard that you want to start a new restaurant? I have never heard of someone so young starting this type of project. Tell me more."

"Oh yea, it is going to be a *halal* restaurant that serves American-style food. I really feel like there is a great market for it, so I really want to establish a business to take advantage of that."

Impressed, Mansoor responded, "Wow, that's really great. What stage are you at right now?"

Kameela again spoke in a whisper, "Actually, it's funny you asked. I picked this restaurant so that I could sneak out of here with a menu. It will give me a lot of great ideas about what kind of food to make at the restaurant."

With that, Kameela unceremoniously opened her large purse and snuck the leather-bound menu into it. Amused with herself, she winked at Mansoor.

Stunned, Mansoor only stared back at her blankly.

"Oh my gosh! I forgot to tell you the best part. I will go through the hardest and strictest possible methods to obtain halal meat for the restaurant so that the Muslim community has the utmost trust in the food that we serve."

Still not sure how to react to the situation, Mansoor merely nodded.

Kameela continued, "So I have decided to name the restaurant *Integrity*. It is my favorite word and will show the honor and ethics that we will showcase at our restaurant."

She looked at her watch.

"Mansoor, can I ask you a favor?"

"Sure, what is it?"

"I really prefer to pray my salaat at the earliest possible time. Would you mind if I did that and came back in a few minutes?"

Nodding, he quickly assented, "Of course, Kameela, no problem."

"Thanks Mansoor! Oh by the way, try not to let the waitress notice I made my own lemonade … And make sure no one no sees the menu in my purse. Be right back!"

\*    \*    \*

As you can see here, Kameela portrays the essence of an individual with a high degree of integrity but only with her words. Her actions paint an entirely different picture and show where her true moral compass lies.

While the story may be an amusing anecdote, the implications of such behavior in a potential marriage candidate are very serious. For example, Kameela seemed to have no regard for the rights of the waitress or the restaurant.

While it may be argued that the waitress and restaurant were strangers to Kameela, this is actually the true test of ethical behavior: treatment of people with whom you do not have a previous relationship. Put another way, a great indicator of your personal moral compass is how you treat strangers.

How Kameela, or your potential marriage partner, treats strangers will give you insight as to how they will treat your family and friends and what values they will instill in your future children. Kameela's story is an extreme example, but in your case, pay close attention to how the other person interacts with strangers.

You should also note that you will be under the same degree of scrutiny by not only your potential marriage partner, but his or her family as well. Treating others with courtesy and respect, even when you believe no one else is watching, will help you give a positive impression to others.

Furthermore, the polite and courteous treatment of others should not be an act or a temporary performance to convince someone to marry you. According to some *hadith*, the Holy Prophet indicated that one of his main missions was to teach the world about the importance of morals and ethics. If you take this lesson to heart, you will grow as a person and increase the regard others have for you.

\*     \*     \*

The topic of hijab is an immensely important and sensitive topic. Many individuals spend a significant amount of time analyzing this issue in the context of marriage.

As a hard and inflexible rule, no male should ever ask

a sister to permanently abandon hijab for the sake of marriage (or for any other reason). Any such request is considered highly offensive and, depending upon the parties involved, may be viewed as perverted and disgusting.

Many Muslims spend a great deal of time thinking about hijab in the context of their lives and their future marriage. Due to logistical and cultural norms, the topic becomes quite sensitive for many Muslim men and women.

It is important that you discuss this topic with your potential marriage partner while making your decision to marry them or not. While you may have either stringent or relaxed viewpoints on the topic, it is impossible for the other party to guess what your thoughts are unless you tell them.

Regardless of your stance on the topic, you should realize that the other person is unlikely to change their viewpoint.

Sisters who have begun hijab will not cease it for you, and sisters who do not perform hijab will rarely begin the practice based upon your insistence.

Brothers who find hijab important will not change their minds—although there are brothers who are indifferent to hijab and may be flexible as to their future spouse's behavior.

Regardless of your stance, or the other party's stance, a conversation on the topic is something that you should have. The consequences of failing to do so may be serious and far-reaching, so make sure to avoid future arguments by engaging in polite discourse early on.

\*　　\*　　\*

Adherence to Islam is likely one of the most important considerations in marriage. Specifically, the contrast in the level and methodology of faith practices are particularly necessary to consider.

There is no easy answer or solution to this issue. You must conduct a frank analysis of yourself and see what maximum and minimum level of practice you are prepared to engage in with your future potential spouse.

After doing that, you will need to determine what each particular marriage partner is willing and likely to think on the same topic.

Obviously, you will not want to marry someone drastically less religious or practicing than you are, but for many Muslims, the idea of marrying someone more religious is appealing.

There is nothing wrong with that idea. Marrying someone more religious is perfectly fine, but only as long as you don't pretend to be more religious than you are, and the other party is fully aware of your level of practice.

If you do, in fact, marry a Muslim more religious than you are, you must be prepared to make some lifestyle changes in order to more appropriately match their level of practice. This is part of the "package" of marrying someone who strongly adheres to the practices of Islam.

Of course, this is a goal for many. Many Muslim men and women strive to be more religious and believe that marriage can help them do so if they marry the right party.

The Prophet of Islam never directly advocated that Muslims should only marry people who are "more" religious than they are. Instead, he advocated that Muslims marry individuals who help each other strive in the way of Islam. There are a few ways of interpreting this *hadith*. One way of viewing this tradition is the understanding that it is perfectly acceptable to marry someone of equal religious practice, or even slightly lesser religious practice, as long as there is the understanding that you will both help each other to try to become better Muslims. Of course, this goal must be taken within reason, as discussed in later paragraphs. Some change is entirely likely and realistic, but expecting drastic change may leave you wanting.

*     *     *

It has become increasingly common for young Muslims to pursue marriage out of an unusual sense of misplaced duty, such that they believe that they are required by Islam to marry an individual so as to teach that person religious beliefs.

Put another way, some Muslims seek marriage on the basis of feeling that it is their duty to marry a less religious person so that they can teach that person about Islam.

This way of thinking is completely foreign to Islam and has never been suggested by any reputable source since the life of the Holy Prophet continuing on into modern times.

There is not even the slightest suggestion that Islam recommends, much less requires, that you marry a person so as to become their religious guide or to ensure that they fulfill the precepts of Islam.

This concept actually contradicts the basic and fundamental teaching that each Muslim is only responsible for him or herself and earns rewards and sins only as a consequence of their own actions.

To be clear, if you simply want to marry a person, and, additionally you want to teach them about Islam, or learn about Islam from them, there is absolutely nothing wrong with this.

It is entirely your decision, which is the point of this discussion—there is no requirement or recommendation that you must marry a person who is lacking in faith so as to "upgrade" them into being a better Muslim.

In general, you must be prepared to accept the person you are choosing for marriage to substantially remain the same, whether it is in regard to religious issues or not.

It is unrealistic to expect someone to change in a drastic way after marriage. This remains true even if the other party promises to change a specific thing about their personality.

For example, an individual who has never prayed or fasted before marriage cannot realistically be expected to studiously begin praying or fasting during marriage.

The idea that a person will perform the obligatory

aspects of Islam for your sake, and not otherwise, should give you pause, and you should reflect on how realistic these changes are likely to be.

In the same way, an individual with personality traits unrelated to the specific practice of Islam will maintain those personality traits during marriage. This means that potential marriage candidates with undesirable personality traits will behave the same way during marriage.

Therefore, it is recommended that you avoid marrying a person who, in your view, is a "fixer upper." Do not marry anyone who you believe you will need to rehabilitate to become a compatible marriage partner.

Not only is it unlikely that you will succeed, you will cause yourself and that person undue stress, confusion, and resentment that could have been prevented if you had simply realized that marriage does not cause a personality-altering change in anyone's life.

Another way to think about this issue is to consider, if you are a person with high regard for religion or a person that is light-hearted, whether it is possible for your spouse, after getting married to you, to teach you to value religion *less*—to teach you and convince you to become a mean-hearted person. It is likely that you would not change in these ways no matter what happened and no matter how hard your spouse tried to convince you to do so.

Accordingly, even though Islamic teachings and moral behaviors are important to accept and practice, once a person has committed to a lifestyle and the related choices, it is not realistic for you to enter into marriage and be successful in changing that person.

While your marriage partner will remain substantially the same, please also recognize that change is a part of life.

In the same way that your personality would change from age twenty to age thirty and again from age thirty to age forty, so shall the personality of any individual you seek to marry. It is not possible for anyone to remain the same forever.

The key factor here is that in marriage, it is hoped that you and your spouse will grow and change together in ways that make you more and more compatible.

# Chapter 7

# THE FACEBOOK CHAPTER

Whether it is right or wrong, fair or unfair, haram or halal, the reality is that Facebook, Google Plus, Instagram, Vine, Twitter, and many forms of social media are prevalent in society. The overwhelming majority of young adult Muslims utilize these networks as a part of their daily lives.

Many readers might object to the idea of changing their profiles for the sake of marriage, perhaps concerned about presenting a false image or disingenuously presenting themselves.

This, however, is not warranted. No one should like or attempt to deceive others through the use of social media. However, with that in mind, it is important to present yourself in the best, most accurate light.

For example, in an interview you might wear formal clothing, such as a suit or a dress, despite the fact that you do not ordinarily wear suits or dresses casually.

Does this mean that you are presenting yourself in a false light for the sake of a job?

Of course not! In that situation, just as in this one, you are simply making every effort to present yourself in the best possible light.

It is also a fact that privacy controls on social media websites are perpetually becoming more and more loose. A picture that might be private today could be public tomorrow.

Regardless of what privacy filters are set up, this book will offer you a methodology on how to help you use social media networks to your advantage.

## STEP 1: THE PROFILE PICTURE OR "FACEBOOK STALKING"

The most noticeable aspect of Facebook and other social media websites is the profile picture. Usually it can be seen by anyone, regardless of whether they are connected to you or not. Accordingly, this is one of the most important sections for you to have control over.

In the process of becoming married, at some point, the other person will see you before they interact with you, and so the first impression you make on another individual is visual.

If the interaction happens in person, your appearance on that particular day will contribute to how you are perceived, but if the interaction happens digitally, you can control the perception directly.

The first and most common problem arises when you maintain a series of profile pictures that you find funny, sarcastic, politically motivated, unusual, or fun in some other way. While you do have the right to self-expression, it is advised that you delete each and every one of these pictures.

\*　　\*　　\*

"Yea, dude, her name is Kiran or something. My folks are going to get her contact information this weekend, and then I'll send her an email, I guess," Junaid told his college roommate, Nabeel.

Junaid's parents had suggested Kiran to Junaid recently, and Junaid was quite excited about the prospect, despite the disinterested manner he tried to present to Nabeel.

Nabeel, on the other hand, wasn't having it.

"Come on man, we both know you are probably on your fifth draft of the email you are going to send her. I know you probably had your English professor look it over. "

Both roommates had a laugh at the good-natured teasing. Junaid quietly realized, however, that Nabeel was right in a sense.

He really wanted to make a good impression on Kiran. And his English professor gave some great tips, although he also gave Junaid some funny looks when first approached about the matter.

"Dude! You gotta look at my new profile picture—it's freaking hilarious!" Junaid chuckled between bouts of laughter, quickly switching the topic.

Nabeel walked over and as soon as he saw the screen, found himself uncontrollably laughing.

Regaining composure for only a moment, he summarized the photo before doubling over onto the floor, tears streaming from his eyes from the hilarity.

"It looks like Mickey Mouse is eating that child in that wheelchair!"

The photo Junaid had chosen was from the Disney World theme park and showed one of the costumed characters, Mickey Mouse, hugging a small child in a wheelchair. Due to the positioning of the head mask of the costume, the mouth of the character appeared to be covering the child's smiling face.

While clearly an innocent picture, Junaid's caption

"Giant Rat Attacks Little Girl" was intended to provoke similar bouts of laughter to Junaid and Nabeel's mutual friends.

The two young men high fived one another congratulating themselves on a particularly hilarious joke.

### A few hundred miles away

Kiran logged on to her Facebook, intent on learning more about Junaid before speaking to him. Like Junaid, her parents had suggested that she speak to him for the sake of marriage. Upon hearing about his educational background, she agreed, looking forward to the opportunity.

*A girl's got to be prepared*, she thought as she typed in Junaid's first and last name.

The correct Junaid was the first hit.

*Interesting, no privacy controls*, Kiran mused. *He must not have fixed his settings after Facebook changed their privacy policy for the billionth time this year.*

As she clicked through to his Facebook page, she immediately noticed his profile picture.

"Giant Rat Attacks Little Girl. Lol #FAIL!

#childhoodruined    #mouse    #killer    #killermouse
#disneyland #hilarious"

*Giant rat attacks little girl?*

She stared at the picture for a few moments.

*I guess I can give up on the hope that I'll be having real intellectual conversations with this guy.*

Kiran closed the window in her browser.

*I'll be polite for a few emails, but I guess this really wasn't meant to be.*

\*      \*      \*

These types of profile pictures accomplish only one thing—they lower expectations that people have for you in a negative way.

When others perform a search to ascertain what kind of individual you are, they will draw immediate conclusions from the types of photos you have uploaded. Humor is a personalized subject, and so it will likely be the case that others will not find the same type of humor in pictures as you have done.

Others may find the picture as humorous as you do but may make conclusions on your personality and character, assuming that the topic of the picture has exaggerated importance in your life.

While you can maintain any profile picture you want, you are possibly encouraging excellent potential marriage partners to avoid you as a candidate if you have the wrong type of profile picture.

Group or "wild" pictures of you can cause the same problems. In pictures where multiple individuals are present, there will be increased confusion as to which person in the picture is actually you and who should be taken into consideration.

Others in the picture may cause viewers to make opinions about you based upon the appearance and reputation of the other people in the picture.

Each of these factors can also come together in a way that does not benefit you. For example, a potential marriage candidate may view a picture of you where you are with a group of people. He or she may confuse you for one of the other people and decide against you.

Even worse, the viewer could make the wrong determination and associate your name with the wrong person and wish to proceed in further marriage conversations on this false perception. This scenario is not easily reconcilable and may cause any future talks to break down.

Both scenarios do more harm to you than good. In both cases, someone that you might otherwise be interested in has already become unavailable because of a misperception that you have caused.

The solution is to post profile pictures wherein you are the only person in the photo and you are not doing something unusual or easily misinterpreted.

This does not mean that you must find the most elegant clothing you own, go to a portrait studio, and pose for photos for the sake of your profile picture. You can still be yourself, and you can still upload normal photos as long as you take care to avoid the mistakes above.

The best kind of photo is one that presents you in a respectful manner in a normal scenario. Situations where you can draw appropriate profile pictures from may be wedding parties, functions at your local mosque, social events, and school graduations—the list can go on and on.

Your goal should be to find some profile pictures that present you in the best possible light.

## STEP 2: YOUR PROFILE

Hameed searched for Nasreen's profile. His mother had told him that she had spoken to Nasreen's parents, and they might be a good match.

*She's not going to make this easy, is she?* Hameed thought to himself as he realized that Nasreen had updated her privacy controls, preventing him from directly accessing much of her profile.

*The profile picture is a nice picture, but you don't marry a picture, you marry a person.*

After some time, Hameed had gained a bit more knowledge about Nasreen—mostly innocuous information, but it gave Hameed a clearer image of Nasreen's personality.

*Alright, last link to check and then I think I'm done … it appears to be a Facebook note or something.*

*Click*

"Hey friends, a poem for you:

The rose withers away,
As each petal falls it decays,
Turns black, and withers away,
Just like my heart.

In case you haven't heard, I just got dumped by the love of my life. Apparently he thinks I have "anger issues." Honestly, I swear … I was just kidding about keying his car. What a loser. He didn't have to call the cops.

So … after crying myself to sleep all week, I've made a decision. I'm just going to marry the first guy that comes along and let my parents do the picking. Honestly, who cares?"

*Oh my god, this goes on for pages!* Hameed thought, enthralled by the ridiculous post. *Maybe it's a joke?*

He scrolled to the end.

"So, I'm really going to do it. Sure it'll be a stiff, boring life, but I'm sure ol' Hammy will be a good provider."

*Hammy? …*

*…*

*… Is she talking about me?*

\* \* \*

Facebook and social media profiles can be damaging if you put the wrong kind of information on there. Personal or private information, even with the most stringent of privacy controls, is almost always subject to discovery.

In general, a good rule of thumb is to never post something online that you wouldn't want your friends, family, coworkers, and strangers to see.

Many news reports have indicated that these social networking websites are very open about the fact that they share your private information with companies and law enforcement agencies.

Oftentimes such policies are clearly spelled out in the website's "Terms of Service" (those long blocks of text that no one reads but clicks "I have read and understood this" anyway).

Here, Nasreen is posting stuff she certainly shouldn't be posting. Frankly, Nasreen does not seem like the kind of person who should be considering marriage at all at this time. Luckily, Hameed found out the real story before things got any further.

Make sure you monitor your content and postings for items that could turn away potential marriage candidates.

## STEP 3: YOUR HISTORY

Each of the previous steps should be applied to your history of posts as well. It is highly recommend that you sit at your laptop or computer one day and take some time to scrub out any inappropriate or potentially embarrassing posts, pictures, notes, or anything of the kind.

If you feel strongly about saving a particular item, simply save the relevant file to your hard drive for personal viewing at a later time. In this way you will do yourself a big favor by presenting yourself in the most favorable light.

Do not be afraid to go all the way to the beginning of your account. Rest assured that marital candidates researching you will not give up at a certain point and not look past a certain time period. Anything and everything about you is "fair game" for a potential candidate to find out about.

While it is likely that you can explain any posts easily and without controversy, you should ensure that you have every opportunity to bring up the issue and explain it yourself. The alternative would be that the potential marriage partner might find out on their own and reject you before you have a chance to explain yourself.

## STEP 4: YOU SHOULD BE RESEARCHING TOO

In case you haven't thought if it yourself, please realize that you can do similar sorts of research and analysis. Unlike our examples, however, please try to take whatever you see in context.

It is not inappropriate or unusual to use whatever tools everyone else is using to ascertain information about someone before you meet them.

It is strongly advised to make sure to not go overboard, as there is a difference between researching a candidate and obsessively searching for information that is neither relevant nor available.

Researching someone through the use of social media should never be more than a secondary tool in determining the question of marriage.

In fact, oftentimes the information is not negative at all, and your research may lead to a fruitful and happy marriage.

# Chapter 8

# CONVERSATION PREPARATION STRATEGIES

Before you get to the stage where you are talking to someone for the sake of marriage, it is important that you understand what topics are appropriate to talk about and which ones are best to avoid.

It is often the case that young Muslims seeking to get married are only able to talk about marriage. At initial meetings, they ask overt questions about marriage. Questions such as "How many children do you want to have?" and "What do you view your role as a spouse to be?" sometimes are asked within the first few minutes of meeting a potential partner.

While some may feel at ease with these questions, the vast majority of people will find the questions to be awkward and off-putting. This remains true even if it is abundantly clear that you are meeting with them solely for the sake of determining marital compatibility.

While it is important to ask potential marital partners questions on the topics of children, career, responsibilities, and other topics essential to a marriage, it is not always advisable to do so as the first and initial topic of the very first conversation you have with another individual.

Such questions can be off-putting and slow the development of a natural relationship.

Of course there are other taboo types of conversation that are best saved for a later date. This chapter will attempt to explain the best, and for your reference, the worst topics of conversation when speaking with a potential marriage partner.

The final step before you begin approaching people to talk to them about marriage is to prepare what you will actually talk about. Many young, single Muslims find themselves unable to come up with casual or easy-going conversation and get in the trap of talking about nothing at all, or worse yet, not talking at all.

While you should certainly talk about the topic of marriage directly, you must also show adeptness in casual conversation and depth of character.

\*     \*     \*

Majid's palms were sweaty. He wasn't sure what to

talk about and was running out of ways to talk about how nice it was outside. Suddenly an idea came to him.

"So tell me about yourself."

*Clever*, Majid thought. *Now she'll be able to fill in the gaps in conversation.*

However, as Majid's companion began speaking, Majid found himself lost in thought. He thought about how nice it would be if the marriage with his lunch companion would take place and all the interesting places they would visit.

She stopped talking. *Oops! I wasn't listening. Maybe I'll just nod and that will encourage her to continue*, Majid opined. It seemed to work, and the sister across the table continued talking. Majid was vaguely aware of the topic—she was talking about her work.

"So you really enjoy it, don't you?"

*A shot in the dark*, Majid mused. *But what else could I possibly say? I don't even know what kind of job she does. Biology? Chemistry? Engineering? Social science? ... Wait, was she telling me she is a scientist or that she is related to one? Oh no, she seems to be done.*

Majid took a large bite of his sandwich, hoping to use

the time to think of a conversation topic. *Maybe the direct approach?* he thought.

"So, what kind of person would you like to marry, in general?"

"That's an interesting question, Majid. I've thought about it a lot, and I guess from a religious perspective, I'm more of a moderate."

Nodding, Majid agreed.

"I think I am too. I mean, for me personality is the most important thing in a marriage. Character, morals, ethics, they all come from personality."

*Wow!* Majid thought, *We are really talking now!*

He seemed to be saying the right thing as his dinner companion nodded, prompting him to continue.

"I even know lots of non-Muslims that have great personalities: Christians, atheists, and so forth."

The sister was visibly confused, so Majid attempted to explain.

"Oh don't get me wrong, I want to marry a Muslim."

*Great recovery Majid—that could have gotten awkward.*

"I'm just saying that if I can't find a Muslim, there are lots of great Christians out there too."

*Why did I just say that?*

"Excuse me? What do you mean?"

*Ok Majid, just explain that you meant something else, and you'll be fine.*

"Well, I am most focused on personality, so that's what I want to choose my wife based upon."

The sister appeared to understand his point, so Majid continued.

"Sometimes non-Muslims have better personalities than our own people, so I'm willing to consider other options."

*Why do I keep coming back to this?*

"Is there something wrong with my personality?" the sister asked, clearly troubled by what she was hearing.

Majid knew he was saying all the wrong things, but could not figure out how to correct himself.

"No, of course not. I find your personality to be kind and well- mannered."

She nodded, somewhat assuaged.

"I just meant that if you didn't have a good personality, I wouldn't mind finding someone else of another religion."

She got up, without a word, and began walking away.

"Wait, I just meant I don't mind if you aren't Muslim at all! I'm very open to this sort of thing …"

The sister sped up her pace, steadfastly refusing to acknowledge Majid's pleas.

\*　　\*　　\*

Majid, at no point, had any intention of marrying a non-Muslim woman. To be truthful, he never had any intention of getting involved in that zany conversation. The problem, however, was that Majid got into a conversation about an unusual topic because he did not know what to talk about.

There are many young Muslims who get into similarly absurd conversations because they do not know what to talk about early on in the process.

Of course, as you get to know the other person and their personality, you can talk about more hypothetical or obscure topics. Speaking about such topics early on, however, is a sure way to get into a precarious situation and prematurely end consideration with a potential marriage partner.

The topics that are the most appropriate and 'safest' to talk about are ongoing community and current events. This requires a working knowledge about what is happening in your own community, so it is best to do some preparation.

Oftentimes, there is the desire to engage in conversation on serious topics at the earliest possible stage. While these topics are important to discuss, it is advised that these subjects be discussed when you are more comfortable with the other person, and equally as important, when they are more comfortable with you.

For current events, the preparation is relatively simple: just read the newspaper or a news website. Keeping on top of regular news that is happening domestically and internationally is a useful conversational tool.

Frequently, a news story is popular merely because many people are discussing the topic. When you read the news, attempt to ascertain both what the popular and controversial viewpoints are.

In Western culture, it is quite normal to attempt to debate any news topic by playing devil's advocate wherein you espouse a viewpoint that is not necessarily your own merely for the sake of conversation. While tempting and normal to do so with friends, it is not the best thing to do when getting to know someone for the first time.

Keep in mind, they are also trying to get to know you and anything that hides your true beliefs and personality only confuses the other person. Usually it's in a way that does not benefit you, so be wary of unintentionally becoming a devil's advocate.

One type of conversation that is best saved for later in your discussions are topics related to unrelated hypothetical questions and scenarios (similar to the one poor Majid got himself embroiled in). If Majid had never brought up the hypothetical scenario, the awkward discussion would have never happened.

In application to conversations you might have with a potential marriage partner, you never want to bring up a discussion topic that does not apply to a realistic circumstance and that may be easily confused by the person you are speaking with. For example, hypothetical scenarios involving controversial behavior are best avoided in early conversations.

When you discuss a news topic or story with a potential marriage partner, it is best to avoid the adoption of a controversial viewpoint and to engage in less dramatic or potentially argument-causing conversations.

Discussions about upcoming events that you are interested in participating in are optimal conversation topics.

Speaking about issues that the other person is aware of helps ease the flow of conversation, as neither party has a distinct advantage or disadvantage in the topic.

Upcoming religious programs at your local center or in your community may be fruitful conversation topics. Attendance at the next regional or national Islamic conference may be a great way to build a sense of rapport with a conversation partner.

It is important to engage in these types of conversations, not for the sake of discussing current events and news stories, but for a more important purpose. Individuals in the West socialize by engaging in this type of small talk and use these conversations as a trust-building mechanism.

As two individuals begin to trust each other, the stress and awkwardness of the initial meeting is dramatically reduced.

If you can demonstrate the ability to engage in light, polite, discourse on general topics, it will demonstrate to your potential marriage partner that you have the ability to engage in regular conversation.

It will further demonstrate that you maintain a "normal" personality and will alleviate any concerns of social awkwardness.

This is important. Every person has a unique personality, and every individual has some viewpoint that can be easily misunderstood by others. Initial meetings are governed by a balance of intrigue as to the other person's behaviors and worries about unusual aspects.

It is your job to create a baseline of easy conversation upon which to build a potential relationship.

After you establish a normal repertoire of conversation with a potential marriage partner, then you can move on to more in-depth topics and engage in conversations that are more central to your personality.

The above-listed conversation topics are not an exhaustive list—nor are they a set of rules that must govern the entire relationship.

After you and your potential marriage partner have passed forward from the initial awkwardness, it then becomes appropriate for you to talk about your viewpoints that are unique to your personality or to engage in serious debates about events around the world.

Throughout the relationship, and enduring into your marriage, there is one topic of conversation that is both easy and a bad idea—talking about other people.

Before any other considerations, Islam is strongly opposed to any conversation that impinges on the reputation or characteristics of any other Muslim.

A private conversation between two individuals is not exempt from this rule, and so care must be taken to avoid negatively speaking about any fellow members of your faith.

Of course, there is a practical consideration to this religious doctrine. Talking about other people is a sign of "un-classy" behavior (to borrow a Western euphemism).

It is an undeniable reality that if anyone is focused on talking about other individuals incessantly, you will likely come to believe that this person will talk about you when you aren't around.

Further, you'll be fairly convinced that what they are saying about you is equally negative to the types of things you hear about others.

In a related corollary, if you ever utter the phrase "He

is like a brother to me" or "She is like a sister to me." you will likely set off an immediate red flag with whomever you are speaking to.

Islam does not maintain a system wherein you can simply declare a close friend of the opposite gender, who is unrelated to you, to be akin to family.

If you are male, you can't decide that an unrelated girl is now your "sister"; and if you are female, you can't decide that a male is so familiar to you that he is now your "brother." Islam does not allow this sort of relationship modification, and neither does any other culture in the history of the world.

Religion aside, such comments are often going to be misinterpreted as a subtle reference to other marital interests—even if that's not truly the case.

Your goal when speaking with others for the sake of marriage is to present the best possible version of yourself. This can easily be done without discussing, or even "putting down," other individuals.

You never want to enter a marriage based upon winning a competition of close comparisons. Instead, it is much more preferable to enter marriage with a mutual understanding of one another that serves as the basis for respect of one another.

Put more simply, you want someone to marry you for who you are, not because of the personality or aspects of a third party.

*   *   *

Some people are naturally chatty. Others are naturally quiet. Regardless of where you fall on this spectrum, it is advantageous to approach a ratio where you speak about half the time.

This is not a hard and fast rule, but if you find yourself at an extreme percentage of either talking or remaining quiet, this may be a sign to you, or to the other person, that there is a serious issue of compatibility.

Speaking is equally important as listening. Speaking affords you the opportunity to showcase your personality, including what your likes and dislikes are. It enables the other person to understand vital aspects of who you are.

Listening is important for the same reason, as you gain valuable insight regarding the other person's lifestyle and interests.

When you do talk to another individual, you will find yourself wanting to ask many questions of the other person in order to learn more about them.

Many questions are fair game and will be responded to earnestly and with an attempt to seriously demonstrate core personality aspects.

Other questions may not be so easy to get a straightforward response to.

For example, if you have a direct question about some aspect of marriage, the other party may feel flustered in responding or may attempt to give an answer that they feel they "should" say in order to preserve their reputation if things may not work out.

In such situations, it is sometimes a good idea to pose your question in the form of an anecdote or short story. What this means is, instead of asking a question along the lines of "How would you resolve a serious dispute in a marriage?" present a scenario where friends or distant family members are embroiled in some sort of dispute.

The level of detail is at your discretion, but you should present your question in the form of advice for the scenario you've created.

"My friends, Frank and Melissa, are having a serious dispute in their marriage over finances. Frank spends a great deal of money on video games … I don't think it's a good idea, but I'm not sure what to say. What do you advise?"

Here, you have asked the same question but presented it in a low stress manner that may allow the other person to more earnestly give their answer. This type of "question in a story" method works for many topics but after time can become quite obvious, so use with caution!

# Chapter 9

# HOW TO APPROACH SOMEONE

Below are presented the three main ways in which you can approach a person of another gender for the sake of marriage. No particular recommendation is given to any particular method. Instead, readers are advised to pick the method that works best for their life and circumstances.

## THE TRADITIONAL METHOD

Approaching another individual for the sake of marriage can be the single most nerve-wracking aspect of the marriage process. There is no standard methodology of doing so, and many different methods are often employed.

The most traditional route is to consult with your own parents and ask them to speak to the parents of the person you are interested in speaking to. From there, supervised conversations of a limited amount and duration may occur.

The traditional method has a few advantages and a

few disadvantages in the marriage selection process. The main advantage is that the parents of the party you are intending to speak with will feel more comfortable with the process, as they will perceive themselves to have a much greater degree of control over how a possible marriage might proceed.

The other advantages of this approach mostly relate to the ability to avoid creating nervous situations, or embarrassing ones, if the other party does not agree to speak with you.

The final, and perhaps most considered, advantage of the traditional approach is that many parties feel that this way of pursuing marriage is most respectful of the teachings and edicts of Islam.

There are, however, disadvantages to the traditional method that must be taken into consideration. In the most common scenario, the traditional method is often used with complete strangers with whom you have no prior acquaintance.

Young adult Muslim men and women receive many similar requests on a regular basis. For some, the amount of these requests to speak becomes so numerable that they are perceived as overwhelming.

In such a situation, your request to speak with another individual may be lost or ignored in the face of many other requests. This is particularly the case if your parents do not have a prior social relationship with the parents of the other party.

Another disadvantage of this methodology is that many individuals are strongly hesitant to responding to such requests.

The basis of this hesitation is sometimes based in the concern that the requester is unknown and accordingly merits little or no consideration.

There are also social concerns as some young adult Muslims in the Western world consider the prospect of a traditional marriage process to be unappealing and disfavored.

Such individuals have made the decision to reject all requests that reach them in the traditional manner.

There are many considerations in regards to the traditional route of approaching another party, and there can be no "one size fits all" answer to which method you should utilize.

## THE SEMI TRADITIONAL METHOD

The next method is entitled the "semi traditional" method, and despite the fact that it has been utilized for centuries in Muslim communities, it has also been utilized for an equally lengthy period of time in Western and other non-Muslim communities.

In this method, when you are interested in speaking with another person for the sake of marriage, you enlist the support of a friend or family member of that person. This support usually involves the friend or family member making the initial introduction between yourself and the other person.

In the most optimal scenario, the friend or family member will deliver numerous positive or praiseful comments about your personality to the person you are interested in speaking with.

The main advantage of this avenue of approach is that it maintains the respectful demeanor and aspects of the traditional method and is considered a socially acceptable process in a wide variety of cultures.

If the semi traditional method is modified to include your introduction to the parents of the party you are interested in, this advantage is redoubled in your favor.

There are, however, a few serious disadvantages to make note of. This method only works if you have a friendship with the party you are requesting to provide help to you.

If you do not actually know anyone who is a friend or family member of the person you want to speak with, you will not be able to employ this method.

The other main disadvantage is that it does reduce the role of the other party's parents in controlling the marriage process. Whether this aspect is "good" or "bad" is not the sake of this discussion, rather the perceived notion by the parents of the other party is the main focus.

It is likely that no two sets of parents will feel exactly the same on this issue, so the reaction of the other's parents is not easily predicted. Some may be unconcerned about pursuing this approach, whereas others may express more hesitation.

It is advised to attempt to have the friend or family member that you enlist to give you an analysis of how each person in the process, namely the potential marriage candidate and his or her parents, may or may not react. This will help guide your choice to continue and, if so, the methods you employ.

## THE DIRECT METHOD

The final way of initially approaching someone is called the direct method. Here, you contact the person directly without the use of any other intermediary.

Just as before, this method has several advantages and disadvantages. Presumably, the direct contact with the other party will allow for more consideration given towards accepting the request to speak with you.

The other person will be able to gauge the level and nature of the interpersonal interaction between themselves and you and make a judgment based upon that knowledge. In the other two methods, acceptance or rejection of the request to speak is often based upon other factors.

Another advantage is that you maintain the most control over the decision and method of asking another person to speak to you for the sake of marriage. For many, this remains the primary motivation for using the direct method.

The disadvantages are easily understood. Just as in the other methods, rejection is a possibility. However, here it will be more direct and may cause feelings of embarrassment.

The parents of the other party retain very little supervision in this type of contact and are likely to feel the most hesitation about this method.

There is the possibility that the other person, or their

family, will feel that you have proceeded in a manner that is not appropriate to Islam.

While this method offers the greatest control, it also has notable disadvantages that must be taken into consideration.

*   *   *

Of the three types of ways to approach someone for the sake of marriage, each are valid methods, but the way you choose must be based upon an analysis of the particular situation at hand and the different circumstances that will play a role in the other person's decision-making process.

## HOW TO GUARANTEE FAILURE

The discussion of disadvantages is not meant to dissuade or discourage you but to help you be informed about the potential pitfalls. It will be your decision as to which set of risks you are willing to take and which avenues of approach seem most appropriate to you.

There are, of course, methods of approaching someone that are guaranteed to fail. Many young Muslim adults utilize these methods in a misguided attempt to balance following Islam and avoiding embarrassment but, in the end, accomplish no realistic goal.

One of the biggest mistakes that single Muslims make is the display of dramatic and overwhelming enthusiasm at the prospect of speaking to someone for marriage. To be clear, enthusiasm is not discouraged, but there is a definitive line of excess which must be avoided.

Such individuals often make several, repetitive, initial contacts with the person they wish to speak to. These communications are at a high frequency, such as several times a week, and are done regardless of the fact that the other person has not responded. Examples include individuals who after an initial contact do not receive a response and resort to multiple phone calls or emails within a short period of time in order to garner a response.

This type of behavior will always be viewed as inappropriate and off-putting. For many, the behavior will be received as indicative of some sort of psychological issue (even if it's merely a matter of nervousness) and will be an irreparable breach of conduct.

Another major mistake that many young Muslim adults make is what is called the "email confession." In an email confession, one party will write an emotionally charged and dramatic confession of interest (or something more than "mere" interest) in another individual.

Such confessions are often lengthy and split into multiple paragraphs. The mentality held by the confessor is that upon reading the absolute and detailed thought process and emotional feelings that he or she holds, the other individual will be emotionally swayed into reciprocating similar feelings.

A common aspect of these email confessions is that the party receiving the email will not have any previous direct knowledge of the confessor's intentions and will be caught by surprise when they receive the email. In such a scenario, the confessor also feels that this unexpected email will have a more dramatic effect that will positively influence success.

Realistically, such an email is likely to be a major reason why another person may not respond whatsoever, not even to acknowledge the reception of the email. Email confessions typically lower the respect and esteem held by individuals of the confessor in a way that cannot be corrected.

This behavior is viewed both as immature and inappropriate by the overwhelming majority of people who receive such confessions.

It is important to stress that the same results will occur regardless of whether the letter is emailed or handwritten.

The opposite end of the spectrum can also be equally damaging to your efforts to talk to a potential marriage partner. Many young Muslim adults will make every effort to appear disinterested or only barely interested, even when they are entirely interested in talking to the other party.

This is done for many reasons, such as to project a particular image or to avoid embarrassment upon rejection, a mismanaged attempt to avoid appearing overly enthusiastic, or even in an unusual to attempt to maintain a particular type of reputation in the Muslim community.

Examples of this kind of behavior are difficult to identify, as the behavior is not demonstrated through particular actions but instead by a general motif of inaction.

Unfortunately, these efforts backfire almost every single time. By projecting an overly relaxed or disinterested persona, you will end up convincing the other party that you truly are disinterested. In such case, they will move on and you will have lost an opportunity to get to know someone that you wanted to marry.

Over time, this type of behavior will result in a diminished reputation in the Muslim community as well.

As others in your community hear that you have apparently driven away other eligible Muslim singles through disinterest, it will be assumed that you are not currently focused on marriage, and the pool of singles will diminish rapidly.

\* \* \*

"So yea, I'll just be taking math over the summer so I can graduate a bit early," Latifah explained.

She was at a young professional's mixer at an Islamic convention.

"That's really awesome!" Faisal exclaimed. He genuinely seemed to be very excited. "It is going to be epic! I bet you are totally psyched and are going to have a blast."

"What about you Faisal, what are your summer plans?"

"Oh, I will just be doing an internship near my house. But man, it sounds like your summer will be busy! Taking a class, going to school, studying—it all seems really interesting!"

Again, Latifah noticed above-average exuberance.

"Yea, I guess so ..."

"Latifah, you should totally "wall me" when you get the chance." Faisal loudly spoke. He had a giant smile on his face and was gesturing in a fervent manner.

*Wall me?*

"What do you mean by 'wall you'? I'm not familiar with that term," Latifah said—although she thought she might have a good idea.

"Latifah, you are so funny!" Faisal heartily laughed for a few minutes.

*I wasn't aware I said something funny.*

"You know! Wall me on Facebook. Write on my wall!"

*Right.*

"Oh yea, sure thing." Latifah responded dismissively.

"Faisal, I'm sorry. I have an urgent errand to take care of—I'll talk to you later."

Without further explanation or dialogue, Latifah walked away briskly.

Faisal stood there, smiling. Latifah was a person he was very interested in, and he was excited to get to know her.

Deciding that the encounter was pleasant, Faisal decided to catch his breath by a walk to the lobby which, for the most part, was empty.

However, when he got there, he saw Latifah. She was not in any apparent hurry and did not seem to be pursuing any errand.

If front of Faisal, Latifah was sitting on a couch with her head buried in her hands. She didn't see Faisal but could be heard murmuring, "Why do all the crazy ones like me?"

\*    \*    \*

Faisal may have been attempting to show Latifah that he was interested in what was going on in her life, but he did it the wrong way.

Faisal came on too strong. He showed an unwarranted amount of excitement about a topic that Latifah considered boring at best (her summer math class). After failing to notice her discomfort, he takes it a step further in a way that Latifah finds unusual and unappealing, causing her to leave.

Here, Latifah might have responded entirely

differently if Faisal had not spoken in such a dramatically enthusiastic way but instead had engaged in easy, regular conversation.

Your situation may not be this extreme or may be entirely different altogether. One of the keys to success in approaching someone is a well-known adage of Islam, specifically that moderation is the key to success.

Showing an appropriate amount of interest in a conversation topic, without being too interested or too uninterested, is the best way to engage in conversation.

The appropriate level of interest will be subjective and will depend on the conversation at hand. It will be important to watch for social and verbal cues from the other party to determine how interested they are in speaking on the same topic. Mirroring their level of interest will help conversation flow more easily.

# Chapter 10

# HOW TO BE APPROACHED

The notion that only one gender can approach the other for the sake of marriage is quickly becoming outdated. It is quite common for Muslim men and women to approach one another for the sake of starting conversations about the topic of marriage.

Many times, the initial approach will happen through one of the three mentioned methods: traditional, semi traditional, or direct.

It is important that you respond in a way that is truthful to your intentions and respectful of the dignity of the party that is expressing interest.

In behaving in a courteous manner, you will prevent any feelings of embarrassment that the other person may feel. Further, you will help to establish a reputation for yourself as an honorable individual who can be easily approached.

For many, responding to a request to speak may necessitate speaking with parents or other family members. This is entirely normal and will be expected in many cases. It is important that if you choose to speak with any such relatives that you do so in a direct manner, and in a quick time frame, so as to respond in an appropriate time to the person who made the request.

## WHAT ON EARTH IS "BIODATA"

Many people are quite familiar with the concept of requesting, sending, and/or receiving "biodata." For others, the concept is bewildering and unexpected.

Regardless of how you perceive the idea, it is common for individuals and families to make strong use of biodata when initially interacting with a new potential marriage candidate.

Biodata is a collection of general or summarized information about you and sometimes includes a formally taken picture. The information includes your name, age, occupation, interests, and a primer on your family. It is not presented in a list format but instead is typically described in a few paragraphs or less. (See the Facebook chapter on selecting a photo—the same rules apply!)

It is not very different from a profile created online for popular singles websites. However, it has been done for decades, if not longer.

For some, the concept of biodata immediately elicits feelings of trepidation and concern. This reaction is not warranted, and you should realize that it is the best way for you to present yourself. In a normal circumstance, you may not be able to control when another person or their family first observe you—in many cases, it might happen without your knowledge.

However, you control what you send as your biodata and, thus, have significant input as to how you are first perceived.

## HOW TO TALK TO YOUR PARENTS ABOUT A REQUEST

Single Muslims are often approached about the topic of marriage, and the role of parents and other family can never be overstated.

Each person's circumstance is entirely different. However, if you decide to speak to your parents or family members before responding to a request, there are a few key guidelines that are best followed.

The most important guideline is that if you are actively pursuing marriage and are interested in beginning immediate conversations with others on this topic, you should speak to your family members ahead of time.

This will ensure that any conversations with potential marriage partners go smoothly and are not interrupted while you attempt to sort out the wishes and decisions of family members.

When you do speak to your parents, it is important to use a respectful tone that indicates that you value their input and advice. At the same time, a respectful tone will ensure that family members realize that you are making a mature decision about a topic that is very important to your future.

Levity and cordiality are important aspects of any conversation you have with family members. These conversations are inherently stressful, so establishing a light-hearted or friendly demeanor will help to move the conversation in a positive manner.

Another key component is identifying the correct family member to approach. It is often the case in many Muslim families that there is a "right" person to talk to about marriage and a "wrong" person.

The right person will understand your viewpoint, consider your request, and after careful thought and deliberation give you a response.

The wrong person will immediately reject any suggestion you make and prevent you from continuing forward without giving any thought to the matter. Speak with your other siblings or relatives to gauge who this person is and craft your message to the correct person.

If you have this conversation in a general context, before you have received any specific request, it will be much easier for you to respond to those who approach you for the sake of marriage.

It is your prerogative to speak with your family members on a case-by-case basis; however, this may slow down your ability to respond to requests to speak.

## HOW TO RECOGNIZE A REQUEST

The question seems simple enough and in almost every circumstance boils down to, "Are you willing to consider me for marriage by engaging in conversation?"

There are only two possible answers to the question, "yes" or "no." Of course, in these situations simply responding with a one word answer is inadvisable, regardless of how you choose to answer.

However, there is no standard way to ask someone if

they will speak to you for the sake of marriage. With this reality, there are many different methods in which you could be asked.

It is important that you resist the notion that you will be asked in a straightforward or direct manner.

The most common way that you may receive a request is if someone of the opposite gender asks to interact with you on a one-on-one basis.

This may be at a social function, an invitation for a meal or snack, or other similar scenario.

Another well-established way that you may be approached is through a friend or family member. This person may have been contacted by a potential marriage partner and been recruited to speak to you on their behalf.

In this scenario, your friend or family member may praise the person wishing to speak with you. They will often give you what they believe to be relevant details about the person wishing to speak to you.

In some cases, they will not reveal whether they are merely recommending the person to you or whether they were actually approached by the person to speak to you directly.

As long as you recognize that this is a realistic

possibility, it should not directly affect you in any serious manner.

Other times, if the other party is using the traditional method, the request to speak may come directly from your parents who were contacted by his or her parents in order to reach you.

Still yet, there may be other novel or unique ways in which another party may suggest to you that they wish to speak to you for the sake of marriage.

That the other person does so in a shy manner, or without being direct, should not be a major concern for you. After all, contacting another person who may simply decide to reject you can be very nerve-wracking. Being shy in this part of the process is normal, and if you can look past that in another person, you might find yourself exploring some worthwhile possibilities!

## HOW TO REJECT A REQUEST

The way you respond must be done with respect and should afford dignity towards the person you are responding to.

This advice is most applicable when you have decided not to consider the other person. When rejecting another person, you will likely have to deal with a person whose feelings are hurt, even if you respond in the most diplomatic way possible.

The best way to tell someone that you have decided not to consider them is politely but firmly. That is to say that you should let them know your decision with kindness and empathy.

This display of respect will help the other person move on and not become overly focused on making multiple requests of you or attempting to pursue you in another manner.

Your kindness is also more fitting with the concept of Islamic moral ethics known as *akhlaq*. Conversely, responding in a rude or discourteous manner will surely cause the other party to be offended, and this will likely sully your reputation amongst friends, family, and even strangers.

Compassion and gentleness prevent such considerations and fulfill the adage that you should treat people in a similar manner as to how you would wish to be treated.

Certainly you would not appreciate a rude or particularly harsh rejection from a person you were interested in, so you should behave in accordance with this advice.

Sometimes, when Muslim singles wish to inform another party about such a rejection, they become so embarrassed at the thought of saying "no" that they try to be overwhelmingly kind.

This politeness becomes so strong and complex that sometimes the rejection is not understood by the other party, resulting in great confusion.

Therefore, while you should make every attempt to exercise tact and kindness, you should not be so nice that you actually confuse the other party as to what your true response actually is.

The best recourse is moderation, which is often the path suggested by Islam.

Your response should also be firm and straightforward. Any answer that does not allow the other person to understand your response will be confusing and will cause hurt feelings.

For example, if you are not sure, or if you are leaning towards a particular answer but still remain undecided, or if you only "sort of" feel a particular way, then you should refrain from responding until you have solidified your response.

Delivering a muddled or unsure response to another party is unhelpful to the situation, as it leaves both you and the other person in a state of limbo.

## HOW TO ACCEPT A REQUEST

Accepting a request to speak for the sake of marriage can be exhilarating. Paradoxically, it can also be a confusing experience.

\*     \*     \*

Farheen was flattered.

Asad had just asked if she would be willing to meet with him for coffee and if that would be alright with her parents.

She was seated with her sister at a community wedding, and across the table Asad was waiting for a response.

Despite the fact that she was quite excited and was very much looking forward to speaking with Asad, she did not want to seem too eager.

She decided to stall for time.

"Why do you want to get coffee?"

He began explaining that he wanted to get to know her and wanted to do it in a respectful manner.

Farheen decided to let Asad off the hook, as he

apparently did not expect the question, and she already knew the answer.

However, she had no idea how to say that she was interested and then how to go about talking to Asad. She decided to enlist her sister to help do the negotiations and to make the arrangements for their meeting.

"Have you met my younger sister, Samreen?" Farheen gestured towards her sitting companion.

"Why don't you talk to her? Here's her email."

Farheen quickly jotted down her sister's email address on a napkin and handed it to Asad.

Asad stared at the napkin with wide eyes.

"I'm sorry?" he asked, perplexed.

"Yea, she's very nice. I'm sure you will get along great. I'm going to go and congratulate the bride and groom."

With that, Farheen got up and left the table, smiling. Once Samreen worked out all the details for her, she was really excited to meet Asad.

Confused, Asad and Samreen sat silently at the table.

*Does Farheen want me to pursue her sister for*

*marriage?* Asad wondered.

Samreen was wondering the same thing but was not sure why Farheen would act like that. Surely, she was not going allow herself to be set up in this manner.

"Do you know what Farheen actually meant just now?" Asad asked.

Samreen shook her head.

"I'm really confused."

"No kidding. Alright, well I'm going to get back to my table now. I hope you enjoy your evening."

With that Asad left.

Farheen watched from afar as Asad left.

*Great! They must have worked out a plan quickly.*

She mentally congratulated herself for navigating the situation in the best possible way.

*This is going to be wonderful.*

*   *   *

Unfortunately for Farheen, she was unable to accurately convey her intentions to either Asad or her own sister. These failures in communication lead to an awkward interaction between Samreen and Asad when Farheen left. In the end, Farheen may have spoiled an otherwise pleasant interaction, and turned off Asad to the idea of considering her for marriage.

The solution in this circumstance and, indeed, in most cases, is to directly communicate your wishes with all of the involved parties.

Whether you respond through an intermediary or directly, it is important that you clarify that you are accepting the request.

If you wish to have someone convey this response for you, specify to that person that you would like for them to respond on your behalf and that your answer is yes.

If necessary, explain to them your reasons for not responding directly. It is perfectly acceptable to use someone else to convey a message that you have agreed to meet or speak with a potential marriage partner, but it is vital that this message be passed on with clarity.

## WEDDINGS, CONVENTIONS AND OTHER PLACES YOU MAY BE APPROACHED

You will have little control over where someone may or may not notice you, but you will always have control over your response to such a situation.

In many cases, you can simply defer your consideration and response until after the event. After all, there is no realistic expectation that you will respond to a request at a wedding, mosque function, or other social event.

(Well, the requester may not have thought it through and might desire an immediate response, but there's no problem in asking for more time.)

If you do receive a communication from a potential marriage partner in these situations, it is advised that you take some time in responding.

The best way to do so is to simply indicate to the other person that you need some time to think about what they have said. Quickly responding "yes" or "no" without considering the circumstance or consequences may leave you with a decision that you regret.

The converse is true at matrimonial or marriage conventions. Here, a much quicker response is most appropriate. Such conventions are usually organized by Muslims who wish to facilitate marriage amongst their unmarried peers.

They take many different forms—sometimes being solitary events and, in other circumstances, being a major (or minor) aspect of a larger Islamic convention that focuses on a variety of topics.

Over time, such events have steadily gained in popularity and effectiveness.

There was a time when such events were considered somewhat embarrassing; however, as they became more commonplace, the Muslim community has adapted, and now matrimonial events are considered regular and normal.

If you attend a matrimonial event, there is some important etiquette to observe—otherwise you may find yourself making mistakes that could have been easily avoided.

At a matrimonial event, it is best advised to not take a lengthy period of time in considering an individual for the sake of marriage.

After all, the expectation is that you attended the event with marriage in mind and are actively interested in interacting with other candidates.

*    *    *

Nafeesa sat at the table smiling. She was getting along quite well with Shahid who seemed to be very interested in speaking with her.

The two were participating in the matrimonial session

of one of the nation's largest Islamic conventions. Enjoying that they had a quick, personal connection and easy repertoire, Shahid intended to respectfully request her contact information.

"Sister Nafeesa, I am very grateful that we had the opportunity to meet today," Shahid announced.

Nafeesa's cheeks reddened. "Thank you, Shahid. You are very kind."

"I was wondering if you would like to remain in contact after this session is over? I speak for myself when I say that I think we are getting along quite well."

"Oh, I definitely agree. I had a great time today, but …"

"What is it Nafeesa?"

"Well, it's my parents …"

"Oh, that's not a problem. I completely understand if you need to speak or confer with your parents. That's perfectly fine with me."

"And I'll understand whichever way they go. Please don't worry about the stress of having to say no because of their decisions. I would not want to cause any friction or anything at such an early stage."

"Actually, the thing is … I've already spoken to them."

"What? What do you mean? We just met and you haven't left the room or made any calls since we started speaking. How would they even know who I am?"

"Well, I didn't talk to them about you. I actually talked to them before I came to the matrimonial program itself."

Nodding, Shahid replied, "Ah, I understand. You received some sort of general permission. Makes sense."

"No … that's not it."

Nafeesa did not continue. Confused, Shahid waited for a few moments before prompting her.

"I'm afraid I don't understand Nafeesa. What are you trying to say?"

"Well, I got the permission of my parents to come to the matrimonial session and engage in discussions."

"Well, so good so far, right?"

"… but I'm not allowed to continue any discussions outside of this session. My parents don't want me to talk to any guys at all because they don't want me getting married anytime soon. Frankly, I agree with them."

Without realizing it, Shahid took a step back.

"Wait, Nafeesa. I can understand if you aren't interested. That is absolutely your decision and I do not fault you at all for it."

"No, that's not it. I really like you—I just am not going to pursue marriage with anyone right now."

"So you were allowed to come here and talk to guys, but you were never serious about it?"

Nafeesa shrugged.

"I mean that is one way of putting it, but I really enjoyed talking to you. I'm sure you are going to find a wonderful wife someday."

"Nafeesa, I spent hundreds of dollars on tickets and hotel reservations to come to this conference. I skipped all the lectures just to be at the matrimonial session because I am looking for a wife."

"You are telling me that you came to this convention, to this singles session, where Muslims seeking to marry one another come meet and mingle and that you had no intention of seriously considering anyone?

"Nafeesa, I spent the entire session talking to you and not anyone else. I could have devoted my time to someone who was truly thinking about marriage. I know that it doesn't always work out so simply, but I would have liked to have had a real chance to be considered."

Nafeesa considered his remarks for a moment.

"Oh man, that's tough. I will make sure I pray for you. I hope you have better luck next year!"

With that, Nafeesa stood up and leisurely left the room. Moments later, the session ended and the attendees moved on to other aspects of the convention.

Still shocked, Shahid silently watched as the participants filed out of the room. Just before the exit door closed, Shahid saw Nafeesa at the registration desk, apparently signing up for the next matrimonial session.

\* \* \*

If it is relevant to your situation, it is important that you have the necessary permission from your parents or family members before you even walk in the room. Such permission should include the allowance to generally consider potential marriage partners without a case-by-case analysis done by parents.

If you don't have permission to be serious in these types of programs, like Nafeesa, then it is a waste of everyone's time for you to attend. While sometimes enjoyable, singles' functions at Muslim conventions are not the place to experiment or disrespect others for casual entertainment. Certainly Islam does not allow for casual or entertainment-based interactions such as this.

Also, if your family situation and wishes of your parents require that each candidate be screened before you can even speak to them in an introductory manner, then perhaps such events are not for you.

For those situations, there are matrimonial conventions geared towards parents or whole family interactions. In these events, the programs are generally geared towards initial interactions between the parents of the two potential marriage partners who then meet and make decisions regarding whether you will move forward or not.

These conventions are not common but do appear from time to time.

However, in the regular circumstance of matrimonial events, you should be entirely prepared to consider candidates on a much quicker time schedule than normal.

Don't worry—you need not make your decision within seconds or minutes, but since these conventions are often held outside of your local city, your timetable should be to make a decision before the end of the matrimonial events of the day—any longer and you risk having the decision taken out of your hands, as the other party may simply leave the matrimonial event and attend other parts of the convention.

What this means is that you should participate in these events with the mindset that you will be required to approach or be approached by others and receive or deliver responses without much delay.

Of course, in doing so, things move much quicker, but that is the nature of matrimonial conventions.

You can prepare yourself in a few ways for such events in a manner that promotes success in the matrimonial process.

## DRESS CODE

In any situation where you expect to approach or be approached, you should dress well. For sisters, the definition of how to dress well is both nuanced and perhaps too extensive for this book. In this case, it may be best to take cues from the advice prepared for brothers.

For young adult Muslim men, what to wear to a matrimonial event can be confusing. Many desire to balance the notion of wanting to appear "casual" with the desire to appeal to others. It is difficult to ascertain how casual, trendy, or fashionable to dress.

The answer is quite simple—wear a suit. Do not wear a t-shirt, shorts, sandals, or any other casual wear. Dressing the right way conveys several important messages to sisters at such events.

The first message is visual: You are well-dressed. Unfortunately, many brothers will attend these events dressed in bizarre and unappealing attire. Sports jerseys, caps, male jewelry, and other "fun" clothing will make an appearance and will likely be judged negatively.

From the perspective of a sister, when there are two candidates and one is well-dressed and the other is not, there is the presumption that the person who is not well-dressed is unprepared for the event and does not understand common social etiquette.

The second message is that a well-dressed individual is taking the event seriously. Attendees at these programs are often concerned with interacting with candidates who are merely "browsing" or are otherwise uncommitted to the idea of marriage.

Dressing appropriately helps alleviate these concerns in a positive manner.

The final message is that you are a professional. You came to this event well-dressed, serious in your attempts to find a spouse, and when all of these factors come together, you give the message that you know what you are doing. For many, this message is appealing for a variety of reasons, all of which are in your favor.

Some may prefer to wear something different from a suit, such as a particularly noteworthy brand name or otherwise expensive clothing. This is done in order to demonstrate a particular style and personality.

While it is your prerogative to wear whatever you would like, please take note that there are many pitfalls to such a strategy. For example, it may be the case that you are not as knowledgeable about fashion as you think you are. Indeed, fashion sense is a subjective notion and may be interpreted in a variety of ways by different people.

Another idea to consider is that attempting to filter candidates through fashion sense is a poor idea and demonstrates remarkable immaturity. That a lifetime decision can be made by wearing a particular piece of clothing, and then gauging reactions to the apparel, is evidence that life priorities are seriously askew.

Finally, wearing particular or unique clothing may cause otherwise interested candidates to decide that you are too unusual to pursue.

One of the main themes of this book is that decisions on marriage are best made by an analysis of each individual's personality and legitimate characteristics.

Put more simply, you should marry (or reject) someone for who they are, and you should allow someone to marry (or reject) you for your true nature, not because of unimportant or unrelated issues.

## WHAT ABOUT CHAPERONES?

A chaperone is a person who will act as a referee for your meeting with a potential marriage partner, hopefully acting to ensure that the rules of Islam and other etiquette are observed. It is good to have a chaperone.

However, it is even better to have a guardian. In this context, the word 'guardian' is used in the Islamic context, not legal. This type of guardian can be a parent but doesn't have to be. It can be any other respected elder or other family member who will behave in a way that encourages Islamic interactions but also serves to protect your interests. A guardian is someone who will be able to recognize red flags and be able to counsel you on a multitude of signs that things are going well.

Choose your guardian well and you will have an excellent experience and wonderful guidance as you proceed through the process of finding a suitable marriage partner.

# Chapter 11

# WELL THAT'S SUBTLE …

Sabira plopped down in her seat, obviously happy.

"Faisal got me flowers for my birthday yesterday,—it made me so happy! I never get flowers."

Stone-faced, Tanveer nodded.

"That must have been nice."

"Oh yea, Faisal has always been there for me. Did you know he's a doctor?"

"Oh that's nice."

"Yea, he's really generous too—he gives so much money to charities, and it is really amazing. I am so grateful to have him in my life."

"I suppose so … it sounds like that is a nice thing to have."

"Did I mention that he is always volunteering?

Hospitals, rec centers, and even Habitat for Humanity. I'm always inspired by him."

"It sounds like he is a nice guy."

"Yea, there's nothing like family, alhamd."

*Oh, thank goodness,* Tanveer thought. *It is some relative. What a relief! I thought she was talking about some guy she was interested in besides me.*

"He sounds like a great guy, it is always good to have someone in your family that you can look up to."

*Wait! Is she telling me about Faisal so that I try to emulate him?*

Sabira continued extolling the virtues of her relative while Tanveer slowly began receding into his thoughts. The more she continued, the less interested Tanveer was.

*Ok, I'm sure this Faisal is wonderful, but I'm just a regular person. I am not a doctor. I don't have the resources to donate bags of money, and I volunteer at the masjid ... not these various organizations.*

Sabira, on the other hand, did not have an agenda. She was just surprised to have received the flowers.

Tanveer, however, believed himself to be on the

receiving end of some sort of poorly concealed effort to change him.

"It all sounds really nice, Sabira. However, I'm very sorry, but I'm going to have to cut this a bit short. I have an important meeting that I just remembered."

Silence descended over the table.

Quietly, Sabira responded, "Sure thing, Tanveer. Maybe we could do this again?"

Thinking for a moment, Tanveer responded, "Sure thing, I'll send you an email. Again, I'm sorry to leave. It was a pleasure."

Without waiting to actually collect her email address, Tanveer gave his salaam and then was gone.

Thinking over the conversation, Sabira attempted to figure out what went wrong. Suddenly, a lightbulb went off in her mind.

She gasped, covering her mouth with her hand.

*Did I just talk about my married cousin Faisal for forty-five minutes?*

\*     \*     \*

Sabira realized her mistake far too late, and it didn't have to be that way. Tanveer's cold demeanor and minimal responsiveness should have been signs for Sabira to observe and then respond to accordingly.

Everyone gives off some type of observable behavior that will help you determine if the person you are talking to is comfortable in that particular line of discussion.

Before continuing, it is important to analyze why you should want to make the other person feel comfortable. Some individuals believe that the best way to get an honest or realistic response from someone is to create an artificially stressful situation.

This strategy is sometimes used in admissions or employment interviews wherein the interviewer will attempt to make the interviewee as uncomfortable as possible. The techniques they use include argument, irrational disagreement, belligerence, or feigned ignorance as to your interests or background.

It's a poor strategy and is usually only used by the bottom tier of interviewers. In terms of effectiveness, the method is rarely successful.

Putting someone in a stressful situation in an attempt to catch them off guard only reveals how they respond to that particular situation. It does not reveal their character, ethics, personality, or any other relevant information about them.

It is particularly ineffective in finding out how a person will behave during a marriage. A successful marriage may have some stressful moments, but hopefully those times are not the majority of the interactions the husband has with the wife. If there is perpetual stress and conflict in a marriage, the couple should take steps to remedy the sources.

Instead, a calm or relaxed person is much more likely to behave normally. In interacting with an otherwise calm person, you will be able to observe how they would normally treat you and others and hint of what marriage to that person would be like.

Accordingly, it is your responsibility to help make any interactions as calm and as normal as possible.

Cues that a person is not comfortable include negative facial expressions, physically backing away from you (even if only slightly), attempts to change the topic of conversation, squirming, or even short or minimal responsiveness to your attempts at conversation.

That is not an exhaustive list, and it may not always be the case that someone will display their discomfort in such an obvious manner.

The responsibility to determine if your conversation is making the other person feel uncomfortable is yours. Luckily, there are some important strategies you can use to figure it out.

Visual and conversational cues are effective tools in determining the other person's comfort level. When a person seems distracted, does not directly respond to you, or seems to be fidgeting, these are cues that he or she is uncomfortable.

However, not every person who is uncomfortable will express such obvious and direct behavior. Sometimes, even if the person you are talking to is completely uncomfortable, you will not be able to tell simply from observing physical characteristics. The clues instead will appear in the types of conversation you have with them.

The best thing that you can do is avoid controversial or inappropriate topics. Such topics are rarely useful for initial conversations and serve as a distraction.

A general rule of thumb is that unless you would talk about that topic with your family members or coworkers, you shouldn't talk about it with a potential marriage partner that you've just met.

If the person you are talking to expresses surprise, shock, or even the faintest hint of anger at your conversation topic, then you might be talking about something that is best left alone.

You will be able to ascertain if this is the case if the nature of the conversation changes from casual to formal or if the other person begins to ask questions directed towards the morality of your conversation topic.

Such questions might include, "Are you sure that is the right thing to do?" or "Why would you want to do that?" These questions are typically asked in a surprised or concerned manner and may be indicative of discomfort.

Of course, context is the most important clue. Those same questions may be asked by an individual merely attempting to make conversation, or perhaps different questions may be asked that do express discomfort.

It is important that you try to realize the difference between normal conversation and any change in demeanor by the other party.

The most effective and powerful strategy to figure out if someone is uncomfortable is to put yourself in the other person's shoes. If you can successfully understand their viewpoint, you will be able to gauge their reaction to your comments in the correct manner.

In doing so, you will better understand the person you are considering for marriage, and you will be able to better present yourself to that person.

The best way to use this strategy is to examine what you have said to the other person and try to examine how your remarks would be perceived by someone who doesn't know any context beyond their interactions with you.

Many times, a person will tell a joke that they find to be hilarious but will not be understood by the other party. The reason the joke fails is because the person telling the joke is thinking about a certain context or situation with various details that are not being told with the joke. Without the appropriate context, the listener does not comprehend the humor and the joke fails.

The same thing happens in many conversations between Muslim singles. The person talking may not realize that his or her story does not make sense because it is missing key details.

This is the guide by which you can put yourself in the other person's shoes. Examine what statements you have made to the other person, and remove every bit of contextual information that was in your mind when you said it to them.

Once you are imagining how your words sound to the other person, think about how you would react if a stranger said the same words to you and you did not have any context.

In essence, your goal is straightforward—try to imagine what the other person is thinking, why they are thinking that, and what you did to make them think that way.

Obviously, it sounds easier than it is, but there is an easy way to practice. Whenever you interact with anyone at all—your family, friends, or even your coworkers, carry out this same exercise. Try to put yourself in their shoes and see how whatever you are saying sounds to other people.

Once you get enough practice, you'll learn a few things about yourself. In particular, you will start to get a sense of how other people perceive you and, hopefully, you will be able to control those perceptions in a way that benefits you.

This process will greatly help you avoid any discomfort in conversations with other singles, and you will be able to better navigate the marriage process.

# Chapter 12

# THE MOST IMPORTANT CONVERSATION YOU WILL EVER HAVE

After a certain stage of initially meeting people and getting to know them, you will at some point decide that you want to more seriously engage in talks leading to marriage.

These talks are more than the simple introductions and meet 'n' greets. Here, you are ready to seriously and directly get to know someone for marriage.

Most people do not know how to take this step. The change from initial conversations to getting ready to make a final decision on marriage is an important process, but it's not always clear how to make it happen.

\* \* \*

Sabeen sipped her coffee nervously. Across from her, Minhas sat on his chair, casually playing on his cell phone.

"Minhas? I'd like to talk to you about something important."

"Sure thing, Sabs. What is it?"

"I'm not sure how to say this, so I'll just blurt it out."

"Sabeen, come on, it's me, ok? You don't have to be nervous."

"Ok, so my parents were wondering when your family will send the *rishta** proposal?"

"What do you mean? To who?" Minhas had put down his phone and was looking at Sabeen with a confused expression.

Stunned, Sabeen took a moment to respond.

"What do YOU mean? To who!? To me!"

"Sabeen, I am completely confused. Why would I send you a *rishta*? We're just friends."

"Friends? Minhas, what are you talking about? We've been 'talking' for six months now."

"Sabeen, we've been friends for six months or whatever, but why would you think we were preparing to get married?"

"Because we talk all the time! Every day! We hang out

at this coffee shop every chance we get. We get along so well. You've had dinner with my parents Minhas. Did you think this was all casual friendship?"

"Uh … yes," Minhas responded hesitantly. "Sabeen, we've never even talked about something like that."

Heartbroken, Sabeen stared at him.

"Actually, it's funny you bring this up. I wanted to ask about your friend and if she's available for marriage."

…

"I think her name is Soraya?"

* *Rishta* is an Urdu language word meaning 'proposal.'

\* \* \*

You probably cringed reading that story. Sabeen made a mistake that many young Muslim men and women make. She assumed she was in a relationship without verifying it first, and in the end she was probably very hurt.

At first glance, it may sound silly to hear that people think they are in a relationship when they aren't, or from the perspective of Minhas, think they are not in a relationship while others, such as Sabeen, clearly think otherwise.

However, amongst regular Muslims, as there is no physical contact amongst opposite genders and the marriage process involves mostly conversation and public meetings, it is easy to see why some people may become confused.

Casual friendship between opposite genders may be mistaken as something more, such as a part of the marriage process. Direct efforts for marriage may be mistaken for casual friendship.

There is only one way to resolve any such issues and that's by having an important conversation called the DTR.

DTR stands for "determine the relationship" and is known by many names. Popular media may refer to it as "the talk," and other sources may use different names. Regardless of the name, the purpose remains the same.

In the DTR, you will have to clearly spell out your intentions and your goals to the other person. The conversation must be direct and will be very nerve-wracking. Starting such a conversation can be scary, especially if you don't know what the other person will say.

Of course, it's important that you do not let fear of the other person's reaction force you to avoid the conversation itself. If you do, you might end up like poor Sabeen, continuing to think that you are in a relationship that is progressing towards marriage while the other person disagrees.

The DTR has three main components that are essential for it to be successful. The first part is the introduction. If you regularly interact with someone, they might not realize you are about to engage in an important conversation.

Accordingly, in the initial step, you must inform the other person that you are talking about something that is significant. This will allow you to gain the other person's complete attention.

The next step is called the disclosure. Here you will have to tell the other person what it is you want and how you feel. This is the one of the most difficult parts of the DTR but also the most important. Until and unless you are ready to talk about this with the other person, you will not be able to get married.

From a logical perspective, it is important to realize that the disclosure is important not only as a way to continue the relationship, but it will help define the relationship continuing on into the future. If you can't tell someone how you feel, or that you want to marry them, you will not be successful in advancing your relationship with them to the state of marriage.

Question: How can you marry a person if you can't communicate with them?

Answer: You can't.

The final part of the DTR is the question. After you have gotten the other person's attention and disclosed to them that you want to start the process of becoming married, there is one last thing you will need to do.

You will have to ask them about their response to what you've told them. Implicit in this is the hope that the other person will feel the same way.

Relaying how you feel and what you want is important, but it's equally important to find out if the other person agrees with your sentiment.

Communication here is vital, and you should be prepared to engage in an in-depth conversation about every important aspect of your life and your relationship with the other person.

You should be prepared to allow the person some time to think about the question and the DTR in general.

This is an important decision. If you are not used to having such conversations with the other party, they will have a great deal to consider. It cannot be realistically expected that they will respond immediately.

Accordingly, you should offer the other person some time to consider what you have said. Optimally, he or she will have been expecting this talk and will be prepared to respond immediately, however, that's not always going to be the case.

The DTR will be emotionally draining, regardless of whether the other person feels the same way, doesn't feel the same way, or wishes to take some time to think about it.

You should make plans for what you will do following the DTR. It is recommend that you find some time to relax, rest, and keep yourself distracted from focusing on the stressful parts of the DTR and its consequences. How you do this is up to you, but watching a movie, going to dinner with friends or family, or engaging in a sports activity are all good ideas.

# Chapter 13

# IT DIDN'T WORK OUT, NOW WHAT DO I DO?

It is unfortunate, but sometimes your efforts to marry hit a snag, and you don't marry a particular person. Perhaps they never agreed to talk to you in the first place or they did not agree to continue on after the DTR or perhaps you were forced to break off the talks because of other circumstances.

Regardless of what action anyone took, the end result is the same in that you are not married and are not talking to someone for the sake of marriage. This can be a depressing circumstance; however, it does not need to be.

The reason it did not work out with the other person is because that person was not compatible with you. Typically the most common reason marriage talks do not proceed forward is a lack of compatibility.

This is not always apparent, and it is important to realize that seemingly tangential or less important factors are actually critical in a healthy and happy marriage.

If the other person rejected you or otherwise ended the relationship, it is because they were not a suitable partner for you. Their personality or circumstances did not match yours.

Realizing that the other person was not right for you and would not have been a good marriage partner is the just the first step in figuring out what to do.

In fact, you will find that it is common for young Muslim married couples to report several failed attempts to marriage before succeeding. This is relatively normal in the modern world, particularly in the West amongst young adult Muslims seeking to get married.

The fact that so many people have similar experiences has made the existence of failed attempts to be commonplace and not controversial.

What you must do, and what every Muslim single does in this situation, is to take a short period of time to steady your emotions and prepare to try again.

When you try again and succeed, any memory of an unsuccessful attempt with another person will quickly fade into your distant memory. Any hurt feelings will easily disappear and will be replaced with the happiness of your successful efforts in the marriage process.

Focus on this part of the process—the notion that you will succeed and become happily married to the right person.

Whether you are rejected or you do the rejecting, one lesson that is important for Muslims is to avoid trying to be friends with the other party. This will quickly become awkward and is often regarded as unusual.

When you do get married, it will be a source of tension between your spouse and you. No one wants their spouses "ex" to be in the picture.

*   *   *

"… and that's why I don't think a marriage is a good idea for us." Farhana finished eloquently and politely, summing up her remarks.

She hoped that Rehan wasn't too upset, but she felt that it was the right decision.

"Alright, Farhana, I am disappointed, but I respect your decision. Thank you for being honest with me." Rehan replied somberly.

"Rehan, I'd like to be friends if we can."

"Sure thing." Rehan quickly agreed, knowing that the agreement to be friends was just something people said to make rejections seem less awkward and not a true desire to be friends. "I'm going to get going now."

"Alright Rehan, have a nice day."

"You too, Farhana. Good luck in the future." Rehan got up and walked out of the room, closing the door to the room.

*And closing the door on Farhana too,* Rehan thought sadly as he walked away. *It doesn't feel good, but I respect her decision. At least we can both make a clean break and move on and live our lives.*

The next morning, Rehan awoke to a text message from Farhana.

"So hungry!"

Confused, Rehan didn't reply, thinking that it was a mistake on Farhana's part.

However, as the week went on, the text messages continued. Farhana continually sent Rehan casual messages as if nothing had happened.

The next Saturday, Rehan had enough.

*What is she thinking? She couldn't possibly have thought that we would be actual friends.*

The notification from his cell phone interrupted him.

"So glad we're friends! This is great. Btw I haven't gotten any responses, is your phone broken?"

Sighing in frustration, Rehan slumped in his chair.

*How am I going to get rid of her?*

\*       \*       \*

In just one week, Rehan went from desiring to pursue marriage with Farhana to wondering how to prevent her from ever contacting him again.

Here, Farhana shows a remarkable lack of understanding of etiquette. After rejecting Rehan, she inundates him with text messages in an attempt to remain friends.

This is never welcome behavior. Nor is it appropriate for the person rejected to contact the other party. The most appropriate behavior is for you to cease contacting the other person.

This is not the same as cutting all forms of communication but instead is an attempt at respectfully keeping your distance, albeit perhaps permanently.

This is true whether you were the rejected party or the one who decided to reject the other person. Any attempts at casual friendship often become complicated, so it is best advised to avoid them.

*   *   *

The best advice for what to do after "it didn't work out" is cliché but true—try, try again.

You will succeed and it will give you happiness.

# Chapter 14

# IT DID WORK OUT, NOW WHAT DO I DO?

It can be both exhilarating and terrifying when you start embarking down the final steps towards marriage, but there are important guidelines to remember to ensure that you have a happy and healthy marriage.

This is an exciting time, so you should make efforts to do everything you can to guarantee that everything goes well. The actions you take up until you become married will help establish a lifetime of joy.

In Islam, it is important to remember that there is no such thing as "almost married" or any form of engagement. That is to say, even though you and your families have agreed to become married, Islam does not create any special provisions that allow you to behave differently with your spouse-to-be.

Two unmarried Muslims must respect the dignity of one another just as they would respect that of a stranger, even if they are engaged.

One of the common mistakes that engaged Muslim couples make is that they let their guard down and assume the marriage has begun. Sometimes, without paying attention, they will make some mistake that puts the future marriage in jeopardy. Becoming too comfortable may lead to lapses that cause your future spouse to actually feel uncomfortable. A misinterpreted joke, unexpected familiarity, assumptions that go wrong, or any one of a plethora of mistakes may become a major source of problems between your spouse, their family, and you (and possibly your family).

While this can be quite scary, there are some simple steps you can take to ensure that the chances of problems are minimized.

The first thing you can do is to simply remember that you aren't married until you're married. This circular and redundant statement is a guideline to your behavior. You should still act and behave in such a manner as to try to win over your future spouse and his or her family.

Do not assume that the marriage is guaranteed. You must convince yourself that you must work hard to encourage your spouse and their family to "agree" to the marriage (even though obviously they already have).

To be honest, this is the strategy you should employ throughout your marriage as well. It will help keep everyone happy!

The next piece of advice is to remember that getting married is not the final objective. Marriage is a lifelong experience—not a goal that you can simply check off of your to-do list. That you have found someone to marry is wonderful, but it is not the end, rather it is much the opposite.

The practical aspect of this goal is that you should not start treating your future spouse with less attention or interest simply because they've agreed to marry you.

Many readers might think that this type of behavior doesn't occur. Unfortunately, however, many engaged Muslims don't even realize that's what they are doing.

What happens is that the process of finding someone to marry and getting engaged becomes so emotionally exhausting that a person feels drained. They may also feel that they have "won" and achieved their goal. Traditionally, when someone "wins" something, they don't need to keep going, and that's the problem.

Inadvertently, many Muslims begin behaving as if they have done everything that they were required to do, and no further action is needed.

Then, either the groom-to-be or the bride-to-be begin focusing on other aspects of life and begin the unfortunate practice of ignoring their future spouse. Regrettably, this behavior continues on into marriage for many couples with heartbreaking results.

In this way, many young Muslim couples find themselves in trouble. The solution is to simply understand what the problem is in the first place—namely that the mentality of "winning" the affection of your spouse-to-be was never the end goal. There are no winners or losers in efforts to become married because the process is not a game.

An effective way to combat the appearance of this behavior, or any other mistakes, is to proactively begin laying the foundation of your marriage.

As the wedding comes closer, inevitably you will be caught up with the planning of the event itself and the incidentals of your life immediately after the wedding. This includes a living space, furniture, managing careers or school, and so forth. It is very important to plan for these aspects, but it is more important to start planning for your life.

Laying the foundation of your marriage includes discussions and planning about how you and your spouse will live together.

These plans include dialogues on how you and your spouse will treat each other, how you will conduct yourselves during arguments, the role of Islam in your marriage, and other related topics.

Conversing with your future spouse on these topics will help you achieve a marriage that more closely matches what you wanted for your future and will also critically will help you avoid misunderstandings that lead to heated arguments throughout your marriage.

This level of fundamental preparation will establish the groundwork for an important marriage. Indeed, this topic is something that could be an entire book by itself.

While this text does not contain significant discussions of what you should plan for, or how to plan it, there are many notable books that do an excellent job of preparing you for these aspects of marriage.

Such books include *Islamic Edicts on Family Planning* by Doctors Dilawar, Saffiyah, Afshar, and Rahimi; *Islamic Marriage* by Syed Athar Rizvi; *Marriage and Morals in Islam* by Sayyid Muhammad Rizvi; *Principles of Marriage and Family Ethics* by Ibrahim Amini.

Important related books include *The Rights of Women in Islam* and *Woman and Her Rights*, both written by Ayatollah Murtaza Mutahhari.

Many of these books can be found for free online or cheaply in print.

# Chapter 15

# THE PARENTS CHAPTER: WHEN WORLDS COLLIDE

If you thought having the DTR was scary, then you may find the prospect of talking to your own parents equally frightening. The thought of talking to the parents of the other person actually may be even more chilling.

The fear, of course, is based on the idea that your parents, or the other person's parents, will be opposed to your plans for marriage. Perhaps they may wish for you to marry someone else, or instead they may want you to delay marriage for some time. Even still, they may have another reason for opposing your marriage that you do not expect.

Oftentimes, however, the fear is unwarranted. Parents may be readily interested in meeting your potential marriage partner and subsequently agreeing to the marriage.

The most effective way of dealing with the fear of talking to your parents is quite simple. Do not wait until the last moment, until after you and your potential marriage partner have agreed to marriage, to suddenly present the plans to your parents.

Instead, the best possible advice is to keep your parents informed throughout the entire process, including before you actually meet anyone who you want to talk with for marriage.

In doing so, there will never be any surprises or unexpected changes in your planning. When everyone is on the same page, there will never be any concern about unpredictable responses.

Of course, sometimes this does not happen. Regardless of the reason why the parents have not been told, the fact remains that you will have to talk to them.

In this case, you will have to have your own DTR with your parents. In fact, the procedure of the actual talk is relatively the same. You will need to utilize the elements of the introduction, disclosure, and question in order to appropriately bring up the topic of marriage and constructively have a conversation with your parents about it.

In some cases, after the DTR, some parents are not in

favor of the marriage. This can be a serious setback and is often a case of major stress or concern.

Here, you will need to figure out strategies by which your parents can be convinced. Such efforts may include soliciting the help of a respected elder, inside or outside your family, who will be on your side with your parents.

Other times, when such a person is not available, another person your parents respect may be of help, such as the imam of your community or a relatively well-known or "famous" scholar.

One of the problems with not telling your parents ahead of time, or keeping them informed throughout the process, is that they may not ever change their minds.

There are many reasons for this. Islam teaches parents to scrutinize the character of not only the potential marriage partner of their children but also the possible in-laws.

In fact, many traditions indicate the importance of examining in-laws for familial or personality-based characteristics, as these attributes can have a major bearing on the potential spouse or the marriage itself. Other times, their reasons may be less well thought out and are based upon fears, cultural concerns, or other factors.

If you cannot convince your parents, then you will have to make a hard decision about how to, or if you should, proceed forward. Like some other topics briefly touched upon in this book, this topic is not something that can be covered in the advice given here. It is a personal and familial decision that must be examined, preferably with the help of an Islamic scholar.

Speaking to the parents of your potential future spouse is a unique experience that cannot be compared to other encounters.

In the initial such meetings, there is significant worry, embarrassment, nervousness, and other related feelings—on both sides.

Indeed, meeting the parents of someone you want to marry is a first impression that can have lifelong consequences for you.

## SCRIPTING OUT THE MEETING

This is the point at which your life and the life of your potential spouse become especially intertwined, and your respective worlds collide.

At the first meeting with his or her parents, many

cultural practices will control the nature and types of meetings. Positive aspects of these practices, that you should seek to emulate, include the tradition of giving gifts, dressing in Islamically appropriate cultural clothing, and accepting any gifts or foods when they are offered to you with a smile and a "thank you."

Before such meetings, it is exceptionally wise for you and your future spouse to discuss what will happen. Will the proposal be delivered? Is this merely an introductory meeting? Who will do the talking?

After you two discuss these aspects of the first meeting with your respective parents, then you should go to your own parents and coordinate with them.

That's right. Talk about what you will talk about. Pretend, behave, and act like this is a movie where everyone has lines that need to be said at certain times and in particular ways.

There's nothing wrong with this and, in many cases, it's even advisable.

For many of the parents of this generation of Muslims in the West, marriage occurred in what is sometimes called the "arranged marriage process." Accordingly, most parents were completely uninvolved in the planning and preparation of their own marriage.

The real life consequence of that historical background is that many parents have no idea how to plan their own children's weddings because they never experienced it themselves.

As such, any efforts that you can undertake to educate, guide, and script out their behavior and actions at meetings with your potential future in-laws will be helpful. Indeed, your parents will likely be grateful for the tutelage and may be quite amused.

If you can successfully and regularly engage in scripting out meetings between your parents and your future spouse's parents, you will be eminently prepared for any hiccups along the way. In doing so, you will most likely have a smooth ride up until your marriage.

# Chapter 16

# LIVING HAPPILY EVER AFTER

There is no magical formula to getting married, and there isn't any miracle needed to ensure happiness.

Hopefully after reading this book, you are ready to embark on an exciting endeavor to find your best possible match.

Please do remember that this process will have its ups and downs. After all, each of the stories in this book are actual experiences that young Muslims have had.

Learn from your experiences, accept them, and then move on from them. Later on, you will find that many of these unusual encounters are excellent fodder for humorous stories you can tell your friends and family.

You don't need to have everything go perfectly. Life is too exciting for that to happen.

All that you will ever need to find the right person, meet them, marry them, and live happily ever after is your intellect and your devotion to Islam.

# ABOUT THE AUTHOR

Rahat Husain is a world-renowned columnist with the Washington Times Communities and with CDN News. With an interest in America and Islam, Rahat is a prolific writer on contemporary and international issues.

Rahat Husain is a patent attorney based in Maryland. He holds a Juris Doctorate from the University of Maryland School of Law, a Master's of Science degree from Georgetown University, and a Bachelor's of Science with General Honors from the University of Maryland Baltimore County.

He is also the Director of Legal and Policy Affairs at UMAA Advocacy. Mr. Husain previously served as the Executive Director of the Islamic Information Center while managing its American Leadership Initiative for Muslims and the Honors Gemstone Internship Program.

For the past six years, Mr. Husain has worked with Congressmen, Senators, federal agencies, think tanks, NGOs, policy institutes, and academic experts to advocate on behalf of Shia Muslim issues, both political and humanitarian. UMAA hosts one of the largest gatherings of Shia Ithna Asheri Muslims in North America at its annual convention.

www.ingramcontent.com/pod-product-compliance
Lightning Source LLC
Chambersburg PA
CBHW071530040426
42452CB00008B/962